STAY AFLOAT

This was me in 1966 aboard the USS *Liberty*. Twenty years old. Just doing my job. I didn't know what was coming. But I'm still here to tell it.

This is my story. Thank you for reading it.

Phil

*Phil Tourney aboard the **USS Liberty**, 1966*

STAY AFLOAT

legal@philtourneypodcast.com | www.philtourneypodcast.com

First Edition

ISBN eBook: 978-0-9601255-5-5
ISBN Paperback: 978-0-9601255-4-8
ISBN Hardcover: 978-0-9601255-3-1

Library of Congress Control Number: 2026906201

STAY AFLOAT

From That Day to Today

by Phil Tourney

USS Liberty Survivor ● US Navy Veteran ● Patriot

My Dedication

By Phil Tourney

Before anything else, I want to thank my children.

Frankie. August. Deidre. Bryce. Shane.

Thank you for letting me be your dad.

I know I wasn't always easy. I know there were years when I carried too much, and sometimes I carried it the wrong way. I know the **Liberty** didn't stay out in the Mediterranean. It came home with me, and it took up space in our lives in ways you didn't ask for. Some of you lived through my silence, some of you lived through my intensity, and some of you lived through the parts of me that couldn't put the past down when I should have.

But you stayed. You grew. You make me so proud.

You forgave me in ways I didn't deserve at the time. You loved me even when I didn't know how to show you love the way you needed it. And you gave me something the Navy and the

Liberty never could: a reason to keep going when I didn't feel like I had anything left.

If this book does anything beyond telling the truth, I hope it shows you this. I know I was your father, but the truth is, you were also a steadying force for me. You anchored me to life. You reminded me that the world didn't end on June 8, 1967, even when my mind tried to live there.

I love you all. And I am grateful you are mine.

Now I want to speak to the 34 men we lost on June 8, 1967.

I have carried you with me every day of my life since that morning. Some people carry photographs in their wallets. I carried your names in my heart. I carried your faces in my sleep. I carried the sound of your voices, the jokes you told, the plans you made, the lives you were supposed to live.

You never got to come home.

You never got to grow old.

You never got the ordinary things most people take for granted. A job. A family. A granddaughter climbing into your lap. A quiet Sunday morning. You were taken in a way that never made sense, and then you were buried under a story that never matched what we lived through.

This book is for you.

It is for the men whose bodies never came home whole. It is for the families who were handed folded flags and half-truths. It is for every shipmate who carried guilt simply for surviving. I have spent a lifetime trying to make sure the world knew you were here, that you mattered, and that you were not just a number.

You were my brothers. And you still are.

I also want to thank the United States of America.

I have always loved this country.

I have loved what it stands for, even when its leaders failed to live up to those ideals. I have loved the people in it, the working men and women, the families, the kids who raise their right hand and volunteer to serve something bigger than themselves. I have loved the flag we flew that day, even when it came down burned and torn, because it still meant what I believed it meant.

Some people confuse telling the truth with hating your country. I never have.

If anything, this book exists because I love America enough to want it to be honest with itself. I believe patriotism isn't blind loyalty to institutions. It is loyalty to the principles we claim to stand for. It is the courage to face facts, even when they are uncomfortable. It is the belief that the American people deserve the truth, because free people cannot stay free without it.

I served my country proudly.

And I still do, in the only way I know how now: by telling what happened and refusing to let it sink.

And last, I want to thank my wife, Lisa.

Lisa, I don't even know how to write this part without my throat tightening up.

You didn't just marry me. You married what happened to me. You married the restless nights, the memories I couldn't shut off, the phone calls, the letters, the reunions, the anger, the guilt, and the ship that never stopped living in my head. You had to share your husband with the *Liberty*, and you did it longer than most people could have.

You believed me when others didn't. You steadied me when I wasn't steady.

You pushed me forward when I wanted to shut down and disappear. There were times in my life when I truly don't know if I would have made it without you. Not because you "fixed" me, but because you loved me through the parts of me that were hard to love.

You gave me a home when my mind kept trying to return to that deck.

You gave me peace when my heart couldn't find it on its own. You gave me courage in the quiet way that matters most, by staying.

If there is anything good in me, you drew it out. If there is anything steady in me now, you helped build it. And the reason this book exists is that you stood beside me long enough for me to finish what we started.

I love you. Thank you for giving me a life after the *Liberty*.

Phil

Praise for *Stay Afloat*

"Phil Tourney is a rare man. He's lived through what most people cannot imagine, and he has the courage to tell the truth about it with clarity and conviction. *Stay Afloat* is a sobering reminder of what can happen when power goes unchecked and honest questions are discouraged. I strongly recommend this book to anyone who cares about truth, accountability, and justice."

> \- **Dr. Charles O. "Chuck" Baldwin**
> Pastor, Liberty Fellowship; Syndicated Columnist; Radio Host; Former Constitution Party Presidential Nominee

"Having Phil Tourney on my podcast was one of the most meaningful conversations I've ever had. What he lived through, and what he's carried for nearly six decades, is heavy and real. The men of the **USS *Liberty*** deserved better than to have their story buried. *Stay Afloat* is a story that needed to be told, and I'm glad Phil is the one telling it."

> \- **Jake Shields**
> Host, *Fight Back with Jake Shields*, Former UFC Veteran & World Champion

"As someone who once supported Israel without question, Phil Tourney's story was a turning point for me. His firsthand account of the **USS** *Liberty* forced me to confront the danger of blind allegiance to any nation, especially when questions are discouraged, and truth is buried for decades. Phil tells this story with integrity and courage, no matter the cost. If you strongly support Israel, as I once did, this book, *Stay Afloat,* deserves your honest attention. Just read it and decide for yourself what you think the truth is."

- **Jeremy Slayden**
  JSlay: Made in the USA Podcast

"The **USS** *Liberty* is one of the most consequential and least-discussed events in modern American military history. For decades, the story was minimized, and people who raised questions were dismissed. Phil Tourney kept pushing until the public finally started listening. *Stay Afloat* is a firsthand account that belongs on the historical record, and I could not put it down once I started. It was a history lesson and Phil's life memoir wrapped into one, and I highly recommend everyone read this hidden story that deserves to be heard."

- **Erik Warsaw**
  Host, *The Erik Warsaw Podcast*

"Phil survived the attack on the **USS *Liberty***. And for decades, he's taken hits simply for telling the truth about what happened. This book, *Stay Afloat,* is proof he never abandoned his oath or his shipmates. I'm honored to have *Stay Afloat* on my shelf, and I'm grateful Phil put this story on the record."

- **Owen Shroyer**
  Host, *Owen Report*

"Phil shared his story at Old State Saloon in front of a live audience, and you could feel the room change as people listened. He loves the country, the Navy, and the shipmates he lost, and he wants Americans to know the truth. We should never let the memory of the **USS *Liberty*** fade. *Stay Afloat* helps make sure it won't."

- **Mark Fitzpatrick**
  Owner, Old State Saloon

Foreword

By Candace Owens

There is a reward that sits on my desk that I did not deserve. In fact, at no point in my life was I even eligible for it. Historically, it traces its roots back to the first commander-in-chief of what would soon come to be known as the United States, then the Continental Army.

On August 7, 1782, George Washington awarded the Badge of Military Merit to three Revolutionary War soldiers: Sergeant Elijah Churchill for his leadership during two raids against British forces on Long Island, and Sergeant William Brown for his bravery during the siege of Yorktown. Lastly, Sergeant Daniel Bissell earned the honor for his successful efforts spying on British troops in New York City.

Although lost to time, we might imagine each man felt proud for having achieved under a leader and for a cause that they truly believed in. Today, that military decoration has come to be known as "The Purple Heart," though the criteria for the award have shifted somewhat; one must be a member of the armed forces who has been wounded or killed in action.

This means that of the approximately 1.9 million recipients of the Purple Heart since 1932, almost half a million were awarded posthumously to their surviving family members.

I confess that I have never been a member of the armed forces, nor was I raised within a family of servicemen. Public school education has bestowed upon me a below-average understanding of military operations. Suffice it to say, a Purple Heart was not foreseeable in my life's trajectory.

And the one that sits on my desk does not inspire me with any sense of patriotism or civic duty to the country that procured it. You see, I inherited this Purple Heart for clearing an impossibly low bar; I merely allowed someone else to share the truth about what was done to him by a country he swore an oath to defend and protect.

In mid-October 2024, I received a letter from a 77-year-old veteran named Phillip F. Tourney. It recounted the devastating story of the most decorated ship in naval history for a single engagement, the likes of which the majority of the world had never heard the truth regarding. That's because the men who survived the attack were immediately ordered into silence.

After describing a most harrowing story of betrayal, Phil concluded the letter informing me that, "USS Liberty survivors are the biggest whistleblowers this country has ever seen. Our only sin is that we survived. We didn't kill anyone. Israel did all the murdering that day, and the U.S. government did all the covering up. I'm asking you to help us save America by telling the world the facts about the slaughter of my mates. We are begging you to support us."

In the days that followed, I reached out to him to see if he would be willing to share his story on my podcast. I remain deeply honored that he agreed to fly out to me in the following weeks.

No words could adequately describe the emotions I felt as I listened to Phil tell me his story in my cramped basement. By the time we finished recording, every member of my small podcasting team had been moved to tears. When it came time to say goodbye, I was certain of at least three things; indeed, God was with Phil aboard the ship that day in June 1967, but He had also been with Phil every day since. And He was with us both as we recorded our conversation that day.

There are moments in life that simply cannot be manufactured. Phil's sincerity, his pain, his moments of deep reverie and reflection. The implausible hurt and betrayal in his eyes were but a reflection of a burden he has carried with him for almost 60 years. And perhaps most incredulously, amidst the pain, an indefatigable hope that lights a fire of courage within others. Simply put, it is a story of a survivor's lifelong determination to honor the perished souls of his shipmates.

"We give all power to Jesus Christ; we were just his servants that horrible day and now."

More than 10 million people worldwide have since watched our discussion. Tens of thousands of letters and comments flew in worldwide, with sentiments of shock and disgust.

How could we not have known what Israel did to these young men?

How could our government have allowed such an evil to take place?

Two years on, and the story that Phil and others have fought to tell for 60 years is now debated across college campuses and is, at long last, becoming more of a fixture in the mainstream news.

"MAGA'S Split Over Israel Extends to a Ship Attacked 58 Years Ago" reads a headline published in February of 2026 in the New York Times. The article credits the virality of my discussion with Phil Tourney as igniting what is now seen as a political litmus test.

What was done in the dark, at long last, has been brought to the light. But what exactly does it say about the state of our political affairs that 34 men were ruthlessly murdered, and one of the survivors passed his Purple Heart to a woman who was willing to listen?

It signifies that we are a nation ruled by weak men.

"God saved us from God's chosen people"

It is still difficult to grapple with the level of betrayal that the crew of the **USS** *Liberty* experienced on that day and for decades thereafter. To imagine a scenario where the President of the United States, alongside the Defense Secretary, colludes with a foreign nation to mass murder their own servicemen is incomprehensibly dark. It represents a spiritual sin on our nation that must be reconciled.

And I have no doubt it will be.

Phil Tourney is one of the bravest men I have ever met. I have made a promise to him to shine a light on the story of the **USS** *Liberty* for as long as I live. One day, I will pass this reward to someone who I feel certain will do the same.

Phil's letter changed my life in ways that remain incalculable. What he survived, what he and his shipmates bore witness to, and this book, I have no doubt, will change your life as well.

Candace Owens

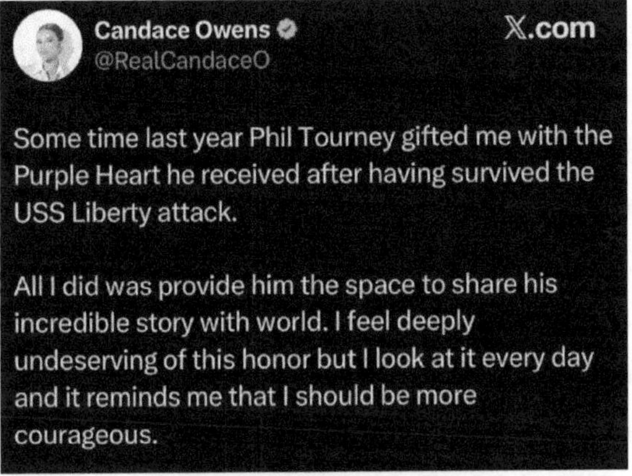

TABLE OF CONTENTS:

Chapter 1: The Day the Sky Fell

I remember the morning of **June 8, 1967**, being absolutely gorgeous. Clear skies. Calm water. The kind of weather sailors dream about. I remember Israeli planes flying over us again and again that morning, dipping their wings in what we thought was a friendly hello. We waved back, proud to see our allies keeping an eye out. It felt good knowing we had protection.

Looking back, you couldn't ask for a more peaceful day to die.

There I was, a 20-year-old kid twelve miles off the coast of the Sinai Peninsula, aboard the *Liberty*, drifting through a morning that looked too peaceful to disturb. The sea was calm as glass. The horizon went on forever. Look how beautiful she was.

The Sinai Peninsula sat between Egypt and Israel, a stretch of desert and coastline that suddenly mattered to the whole world in June 1967. A war had broken out just days earlier. They called it the Six-Day War, because that's all it lasted.

Israel and Egypt were fighting, along with a few other neighboring countries on the side of the Egyptians. Jets were in the air. Armies were on the move. Not that we knew any of this, but lines on maps were changing fast. But out there on the water, none of that noise reached us. No gunfire. No explosions. Just blue sky, quiet seas, and the *Liberty* doing her job, listening, watching, gathering, staying put.

I was working down in Engineering - Shipfitter's Pipe. My rating was Third Class. In plain terms, I worked on the pipes and systems that kept the ship running. A glorified plumber in uniform. My job was to keep the *Liberty* breathing. Pipes, valves, pumps. Anything that carried fuel, water, or air.

Remember, I'm 20. We were all young. Just kids, caught up in a grown-up world without even knowing it. Technically, we were trained for war, not like soldiers, but we were trained. But I was not expecting that. None of us were. We weren't fighters on a battleship. We were sailors on a listening ship. A spy ship, if you want to be blunt. Her official name was the ***Technical Research Ship Liberty*, AGTR-5**. Underneath all the antennas and equipment, she was an old World War II Victory-class cargo ship, rebuilt and painted Navy gray, and now state-of-the-art for the NSA to collect signals. Our job was to listen.

The NSA, the National Security Agency, used ships like ours to gather intelligence. Back then, that meant radios, radar, and military chatter. No computers like today. No satellites doing all the work. Just people, equipment, and patience, sitting close enough to hear what others didn't want heard. Four old .50-caliber machine guns sat on deck, good enough to scare off boarders but worthless against jets.

The *Liberty* herself felt solid. Steady. She wasn't sleek or fast, but she had presence. A ship rebuilt for a new kind of fight, bristling with antennas instead of guns. She rode the water easily, like she knew her job and wasn't in a hurry to prove anything. To us, she wasn't just steel and wiring. She was home. And that morning, she felt strong enough to take care of us.

Our Captain, **Captain William L. McGonagle**, was a stickler for damage control drills, and he was the one who trained us like we were fighters, even though again, we weren't. The crew trusted him because he never asked us to do anything he wouldn't do himself. He knew our names. He knew our jobs. And when he pushed us, it was because he believed we'd need it someday.

Captain McGonagle didn't train us out of fear. He trained us out of responsibility. He understood that when things go wrong at sea, there's no one else coming. Boy, was he right about that. You either know what to do, or you don't. Most of us didn't realize it at the time, but he was preparing us for the worst day of our lives.

I don't know why, but I remember how the breakfast tasted that morning. Eggs, bacon, and coffee. It was good.

Lieutenant (JG) James Ennes, our navigator, JG = Junior Grade, a young officer not much older than the rest of us, was talking about mail call. Electronics Technician Third Class (ET3) Terry Halbardier was below deck, humming while fixing a bad antenna feed. Remember that name, Terry Halbardier.

By mid-morning, around 10:30 am, the first Israeli reconnaissance plane came over—a slow-moving Nord Noratlas, circling us in the clear sky. Then another. Six passes in all. Some so low we could see the pilot wave. We waved back. The American flag was flying, clear and unmistakable. Big enough to see from the air. The weather couldn't have been better. Calm seas. Blue sky. Nothing to suggest danger.

"Friends," somebody said. "We're fine."

Some of the crew were stretched out on deck, catching some sun. Nobody was at battle stations. Nobody was worried. We felt safe.

Most of us had joined the Navy for our own reasons. Some for the steady paycheck. Some to see the world. Some because it felt like the right thing to do. We figured we'd do our time, serve our country, come home, and get on with our lives. None of us thought we were signing up for history.

Around two o'clock, that changed. More jets. This time, a deeper growl. Faster. Harder. Mirage IIIs and Super Mystères, French-built, jet fighters coming straight at us from the east. We were no longer fine.

Then the sky fell.

The first rockets tore the deck open like tin foil. I dropped flat as the bridge exploded in flame. Captain William L. McGonagle stayed upright through it as blood ran down his leg.

On the helm was Quartermaster Francis Brown, who later got the Navy Cross, posthumously. Francis was my friend. We were just two 20-year-old kids that day, joking about what we'd do when we got home, talking about our girls and cars.

He never got that chance. He never got to be twenty-one. I was trying to put out the deck fire with CO2. He was at the helm, and we just looked at each other and shook our heads, like we were both saying, 'What the fuck is happening?' I ran out of CO2 and went two decks down to get more.

When I came back up, Francis was dead.

Francis was dead.

The napalm kept splashing across the superstructure, the part of the ship above the main deck, where the bridge and command areas stood. It was the heart and the face of the *Liberty*, now burning.

Do you know what napalm is? What it does?

It's a jellied gasoline that sticks to everything it touches, metal, flesh, skin, bone, and it burns hotter than hell itself. Once it lands, there's no putting it out; it eats through paint, steel, and people all the same. The air hissed with burning paint and cordite, that sharp, metallic stink of gunpowder that crawls into your lungs and never leaves.

Just like that, every antenna we had was gone, radios nothing but static. Chief Radioman Wayne Smith slumped beside the transmitter, still trying to key out a message while sparks rained around him. I ran for the forward repair locker. Chief Petty Officer Thompson was there, "Take over Tourney," he said. Then he was gone, not dead, just gone. He made his way to sick bay.

Above deck, the jets made run after run. 30 mm cannon, rockets, and more napalm. The deck was slick with hydraulic fluid and blood. **Officer Steve Toth**, who'd been joking minutes before, was actually gone. Only his helmet left, dented and smoking. Dead. Years later, his father, a Navy captain himself, started smoking cigarettes again. It killed him. The cigarettes and the pain of losing his son, and the Navy never giving him an answer, were more than he could carry.

Through it all, Terry Halbardier crawled across the deck with a spool of coax cable, hooking up the one antenna that hadn't been shot away.

He finally got a message out:

"Mayday, Mayday, Rockstar, Rockstar, this is LIBERTY … under attack."

That call should've brought help screaming across the sky because the entire Sixth Fleet heard it. They knew who we were, where we were, and what was happening. At that point, we didn't know who was hitting us. The planes had no markings we could see. No flags. No clear insignia. All we knew was that they were fast, and they were trying to kill us.

My first thought was Egypt. We were off the Sinai during a war. That's where my mind went. I don't think I was alone. But instead of rescue, came silence. Secretary of Defense Robert McNamara and President Lyndon Johnson themselves ordered the recall and told our boys to stand down. The U.S. government knew we were dying out there, and they chose to let it happen.

Then hope. Torpedo boats, three of them, flying the Star of David. Our Greatest Ally. For a minute, we cheered. Rescue had come. Then five white wakes cut the sea. Five torpedoes inbound. One slammed into us amidships on the starboard side, right into the research spaces where the NSA linguists and the Marines were working.

25 men died in one heartbeat.

Radioman Ken Kieffer was blown across the compartment and torn up badly, but somehow, he lived. The blast lifted the *Liberty* out of the water and slammed her back down. When the torpedo hit, I was one deck below, doing damage control with Third Class Shipfitter Rick Aimetti.

The sound was like the earth tearing in half. The lights went dead, pipes burst, and seawater came pouring through the compartments. Then the smell, thick, burning oil mixed with salt and blood, hit like a fist to your face. The torpedo boats shot up all the life rafts but three. We planned to put our most wounded into them. But they shot two of those out of the water as well, and then, in a sick display of another war crime, they took the last one from the water as some kind of trophy.

Rumor has it that it's still in a museum in Haifa. The Clandestine Immigration and Naval Museum in Haifa, Israel, includes the third lifeboat launched during the attack as part of its naval history exhibits. I want it back.

That meant we had no life rafts, and it was just the *Liberty* that could save us. The air attack lasted about twenty-five minutes; the whole thing, almost two hours. They counted eight hundred twenty-one holes in our hull later, more than a hundred from rockets alone. I saw so many men themselves injured, yet dragging a shipmate twice their size out of harm's way. That's brotherhood.

By the end, 34 Americans were dead, and 171 were wounded. Some accounts list slightly different wounded totals, like 174, but official records cite 171 crew members injured.

When the brutal attacks finally stopped, the silence hit harder than the noise. The deck was scorched, pitted. The air was thick with oil, salt, and something human underneath. Captain McGonagle refused morphine and stayed at his post, his leg torn open, shouting orders through the smoke like his life depended on it, and it did. So did mine.

The sun slumped into the sea, and we waited for help that never came. The fires still burned. The wounded were laid out wherever there was space. We counted heads. We tended to those we could. Night settled in, heavy and quiet, broken only by the sounds of pain and the water against the hull. We didn't know the fighters launched from the USS Saratoga had been recalled twice on orders from Washington. We only knew we were alone. That night, the stars came out over a ship that should've been on the bottom of the Mediterranean Sea.

I stood by the twisted rail, the metal still hot under my hand, and looked at our half-burned American Flag hanging stubbornly from the mast. What the fuck had just happened? That's when I learned what it really means to stay afloat. It isn't heroism. **It's defiance.** It's looking hell in the eye and saying, *not today.*

The *Liberty* lived. So did I.

My Reflection…

I'll never forget the young men, the brothers, the sailors and Marines who paid the ultimate price that day. Their faces, their laughter, their courage, they're with me still. Every breath I take is a reminder of the ones who never got another.

When I tell this story, people ask if I still think about it. **Every single day, for over 58 years.** It lives behind my eyelids, the heat, the smell, the sound of metal screaming. Even now, when a plane flies low, I tense up. For years, I thought surviving meant I'd been spared for a reason.

Maybe that's true. But I know now it wasn't courage that kept me alive, it was stubbornness. Something in me just refused to sink.

They told us to keep quiet. To say it was a mistake. To forget.

It took me a while, but the silence felt like drowning all over again. After many years, I started talking. And I haven't stopped.

The *Liberty* went down in every way but one, and I've been trying to stay afloat ever since.

Before I go any further, I need to stop and do what I should have been allowed to do from the very beginning. I need to honor the men we lost.

Look at them.

How young they were.

How full of life.

They never got the lives they were supposed to have. That was taken from them that day. Killed in action aboard the **USS *Liberty***, gone, but never forgotten. Their sacrifice will never fade. We speak their names so history cannot hide them. Today and every day. We remember and honor You. **The 34.**

Rest in Peace William.

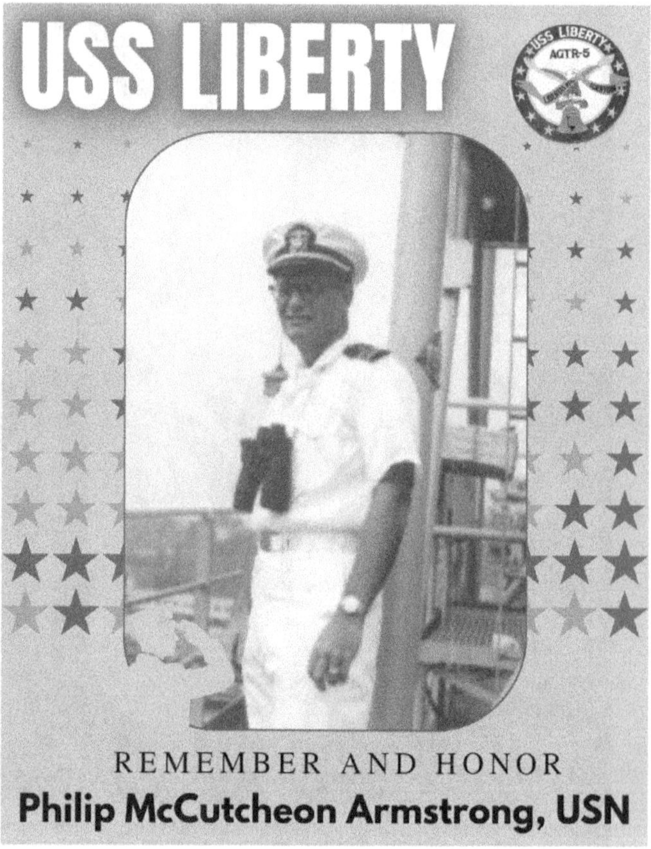

Rest in Peace Commander Armstrong.

Rest in Peace Allen.

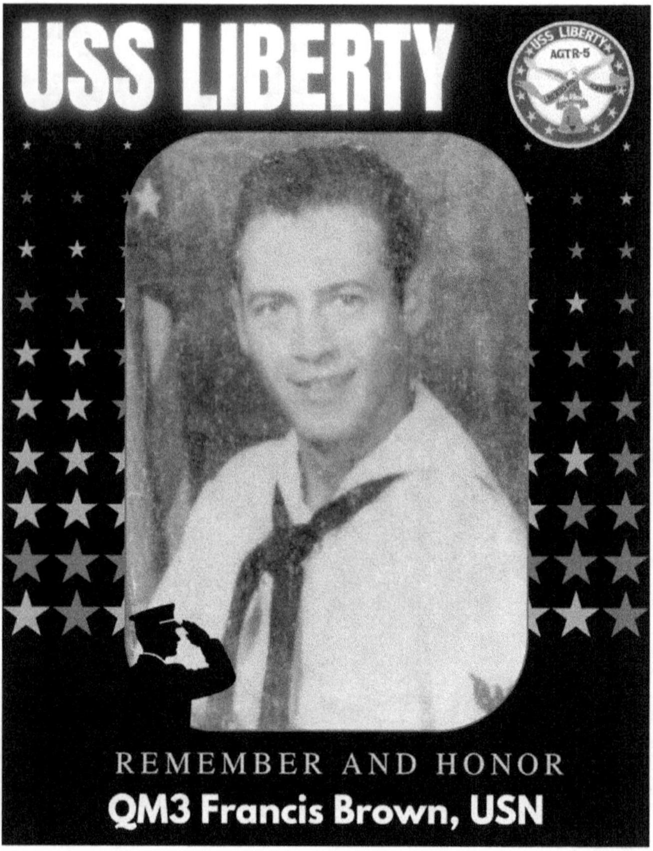

Rest in Peace Brownie. I love you Brother.

Rest in Peace Ronnie.

Rest in Peace Jerry.

Rest in Peace Robert.

Rest in Peace Jerry.

8

Rest in Peace Curtis.

Rest in Peace Larry.

10

Rest in Peace Warren.

Rest in Peace Alan.

12

Rest in Peace Richard.

13

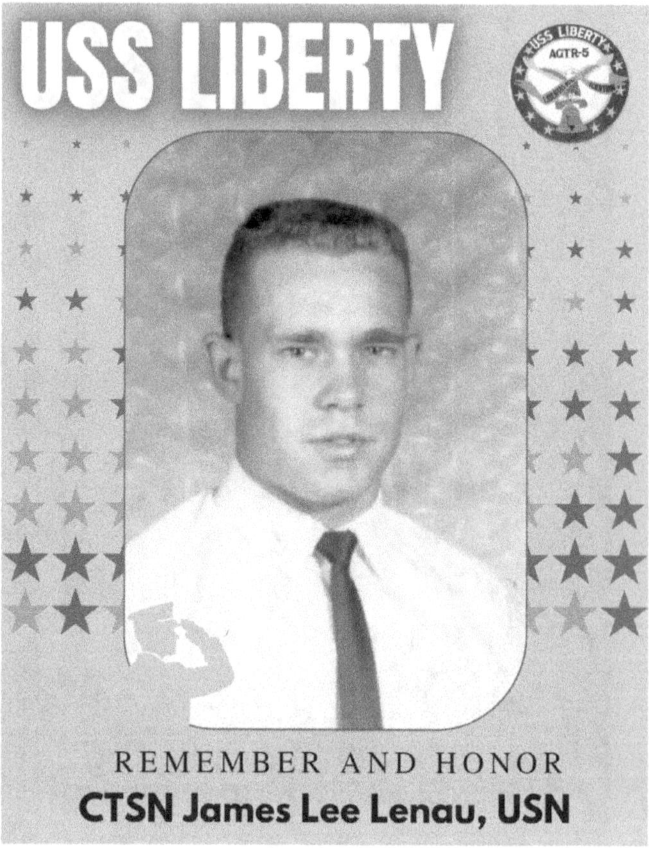

REMEMBER AND HONOR

CTSN James Lee Lenau, USN

Rest in Peace James.

Rest in Peace Chief.

15

Rest in Peace Jimmy.

16

USS LIBERTY

USS LIBERTY
AGTR-5

REMEMBER AND HONOR

CT3 Duane Rowe Marggraf, USN

Rest in Peace Duane.

Rest in Peace Tony.

18

Rest in Peace Carl.

Rest in Peace Lieutenant Pierce.

20

Rest in Peace Jack.

21

Rest in Peace Eddie.

22

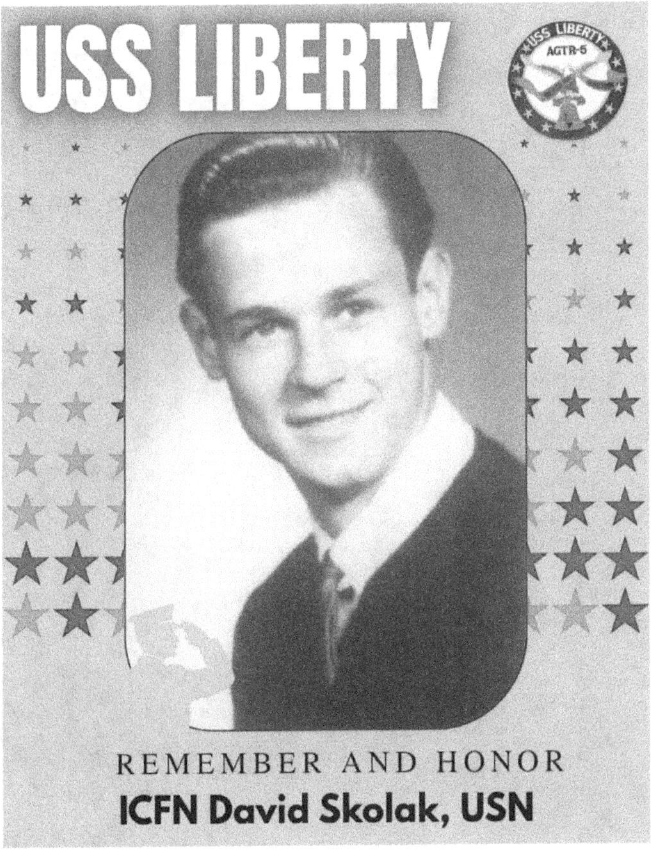
USS LIBERTY
USS LIBERTY
AGTR-5
REMEMBER AND HONOR
ICFN David Skolak, USN

Rest in Peace Skolak.

23

Rest in Peace John.

24

Rest in Peace Mel.

Rest in Peace PC (he was our Postal Clerk. He also ran the Ship Store, so everybody knew him)

26

Rest in Peace Chief.

Rest in Peace Tommy.

28

Rest in Peace Lieutenant Toth.

Some of my shipmates died that day and left so little behind that we can't even find a photograph of them. No face to remember, no real headstone to stand in front of. I'm not ashamed to say it still makes me cry, because it feels like they were taken twice: once by the attack, and again by history forgetting them. Rest in Peace Gary.

Rest in Peace Carl.

31

Rest in Peace. This really kills me not having their picture.

32

RIP Teeky. We used to lift weights together. He was a Monster, and such a great guy.

RIP Fred. 34 Men. Gone but not forgotten.

Chapter 2: Choosing to STAY AFLOAT

For hours, nobody said a word. For hours. We just stared at each other, eyes wide, mouths half open, each man searching the next for an answer that wasn't there. That night after the attack, confusion hung thicker than the smoke. None of us understood what had just happened, or what any of it meant. And most importantly, why?

What the hell was that?

One minute, we were in calm water under a gorgeous sky. Next, our own allies had tried to sink us, and the truth no longer made sense. Even now, more than fifty years later, I still find myself asking the same questions:

What was that?

Why did it happen?

Why did our greatest ally do that?

Why did our president call the rescue back?

Those were the first questions. Then the darker ones came.

Why did I live when the man next to me didn't?

Why do I deserve to be alive?

And the question I still sit with: What do you owe the dead? This is part of my answer.

The details blur with time, but the senses don't. I can still smell it, the mix of fuel oil, napalm, and burned paint. I can still hear the ship's bones creak, the slow drip of water through torn hull plates. The air had a taste to it, sharp and metallic, as if the **Liberty** herself were bleeding. It's strange the things that stick with you. The sound of a wrench rolling across the deck. The flicker of a flame that wouldn't die out. The way the silence started to feel alive, like it was a person staring at you.

We were still in shock. Moving, but hollow. The fires still burned on in spots, licking the edges of the American flag that somehow still clung to the mast. Every time something shifted below, we'd freeze and listen, wondering if she'd finally give in and start sinking. Somehow, she didn't.

The medics, whom we called the corpsmen, were out of morphine. We did what we could. Rags for bandages. Tape to hold them in place. Coffee grounds to slow the bleeding. And prayer. Captain McGonagle was still up on the bridge, leg getting worse, but his voice calm and steady, calling out orders like time hadn't stopped. Captain McGonagle eventually received the Medal of Honor about seven months after the attack, which is the nation's highest award for valor. But it wasn't presented in the way most heroes receive it. There was no White House ceremony, no President at his side. Instead, the Secretary of the Navy awarded it to him at the Washington Navy Yard in a quiet service that drew little public attention. To many of us, it felt like acknowledgment without acknowledgment, proof of his courage, overshadowed by the very silence that followed the attack.

For the next several hours, every man found a job to do. Mine was to patch pipes and stop leaks, trying to keep ahead of the water. Down below, I kept looking at the bunks of the men we'd lost. I remember thinking, *why am I still here?* It's a question I'll carry for the rest of my life.

What a horrible night that was. I did not sleep. Nobody slept. But I will tell you what I did do. I rubbed Gary Blanchard's feet because he asked me to. I was trying to help get his circulation going. I remember Gary asking me, "Tourney, do you think I'm going to die?" And I answered him, "Yes, I think you are." I know that sounds mean, but after what we just went through, lying was the last thing I could do. He ended up dying that night. There was just so much death all at once.

When dawn finally broke after what was definitely the longest night of my life, the sea went glassy again, as if nothing had happened. The sun rose on a ship that looked more ghost than steel. The torpedo hole yawned open, wide enough to swallow several semi-trucks.

One of the guys raised what was left of the American flag, edges burned, but still there. We waited for help. For answers. For something.

Hours passed with nothing but seagulls and static. I used to look forward to those morning eggs and coffee, but I remember feeling like I was going to throw up.

Then, just before noon, a shape appeared on the horizon. Then another. Rescue ships. They came slowly, cautious, like they weren't sure if we were still alive. When they got close enough to see the wreck, I caught the look on their faces: shock, horror, disbelief. The **Liberty** didn't look like a ship anymore. She looked like a floating graveyard.

The doctors came aboard first. Young guys, clean uniforms, eyes wide open. They tried not to stare, but they couldn't help it. They treated those they could, zipped up the rest in body bags, and kept asking the same question:

"Who attacked you?" No one answered.

We all knew, but it felt dangerous to say it out loud, as if naming it might bring the planes back. So, we just said, "Unknown." And that's what they wrote.

Later, I'd learn what was being said in Washington while we were left out there to die. **Secretary of Defense Robert McNamara**, one of the most powerful men in the country at the time, called it a case of mistaken identity. McNamara was the architect of America's war machine during Vietnam, a numbers man, a systems man. He believed wars could be managed from conference rooms and charts. From where he sat, the attack on the *Liberty* was an error. An unfortunate mix-up. Something to be explained away. From where we were standing, burned, bleeding, and counting the dead, it didn't feel like a mistake. It felt deliberate. It felt violent. And it felt personal.

Years later, he'd say, "I didn't believe it was intended at the time, and I don't believe it now."

Robert McNamara never publicly reversed or apologized for the *Liberty* decision. Until his death in 2009, he maintained the line of "mistaken identity" and never acknowledged wrongdoing in recalling U.S. aircraft or in the handling of the incident afterward. He did express deep remorse for Vietnam. He spoke openly about mistakes made there, about lessons learned too late. But when it came to the *Liberty*, there was no reckoning. No apology. Ever.

They weren't all bad. One of them was **Captain Ward Boston**. He was a U.S. Navy JAG officer. He served as the senior legal counsel (chief investigator's lawyer) to Rear Admiral Isaac Kidd, who headed the Navy's Court of Inquiry into the **USS *Liberty*** attack in 1967. In plain terms, Boston was the lawyer advising the official investigation into what happened. He wasn't on the *Liberty*. But he was inside the room where the official story was written. Decades later, Boston publicly stated that the Court of Inquiry was pressured from above to conclude the attack was a case of mistaken identity. He said the investigation was deliberately constrained, rushed, and prevented from examining evidence that suggested the attack was intentional.

In an affidavit from 2004, Boston stated that both he and Admiral Kidd believed Israel knew the ship was American. He explicitly said the conclusions did not reflect their true findings. He put his name to it, in writing. That mattered to us. It meant that somewhere in the paperwork and silence, at least one man was willing to say the record didn't match the truth. Captain Ward Boston said the White House ordered it covered up, that President Lyndon Johnson himself didn't want to embarrass an ally. It's hard to square those words with what we lived through. It's hard to call what happened that day a mistake.

A few weeks after the attack, President **Lyndon B. Johnson** gave a speech about peace in the Middle East. He talked about the right of all nations to sail freely, about the "innocent passage" of ships in international waters. I remember hearing it and thinking, *what the hell is he talking about?*

We had just lived through the opposite of that. 34 men were dead. And the President of the United States was talking like none of it applied. I didn't understand the full picture yet. That would take years.

That morning of June 9, as the rescue ships carried off our dead and wounded, while 25 additional brothers' remains were scattered in the communication space where the torpedoes had hit, I made a promise I still keep. I'd breathe for the men who couldn't. I'd tell their story when no one else would. You don't forget a day like that; you just learn to live with it. Actually, live around it.

My Reflection…

When the sun came up on June 9, I was twenty years old but a thousand years older. Every face I saw that day, I still see. The sound of the rescue choppers, the way the ocean looked, so calm, like it hadn't just watched 34 Americans die.

People say time heals. I don't think it does. You just get used to the wounds. The world moved on, but I didn't. Some went back to sea. Some went home and never found peace again. I carried the story instead.

That's what my life became, keeping their names alive, one day at a time. And even now, all these decades later, I can still feel that moment when the engines of the *Liberty* rumbled back to life.

She shouldn't have made it, but she did. Same as me.

Chapter 3: Brotherhood in the Fire

Before the Navy, before the *Liberty*, there was just a kid from Denver, Colorado, trying to figure out where he belonged. I grew up with calloused hands, a stubborn streak, and a sense that hard work fixed most things. My childhood wasn't fancy; it was working-class through and through. I dropped out of school in the seventh grade to work for my father, trading books for tools.

After dropping out of school, I worked with my Dad doing plaster work. It was hard as hell. I can't say I hated it, but I definitely didn't love it. Plus, I didn't really get paid. My portion of the check went to feed the family. I did that for three years, and any money I did get, I was saving up for a car. I was still working for my Dad and went on the road with him to Sterling, Colorado.

That trip got me thinking.

When we finally got back home, I asked my mom for the money, but she told me she had spent it. I guess she needed it more than I did, but it did sting a bit. Not a lot, but some. But I learned how to work, how to show up, how to keep my word. I remember the long summers, the smell of cut grass, and knowing you just showed up in the kitchen on time, or you didn't eat, my mom didn't call us.

We didn't have much, but what we had was ours. Unlike these days, it seems. I wasn't born brave; I was born curious, restless, and looking for purpose. At seventeen, I decided to join the Navy, my ticket to something bigger than the neighborhood I came from. I didn't know it then, but those early years in Colorado, the long days of labor and the lessons in humility, would shape everything that came after.

Was I running away from my family?

Maybe.

But I didn't care, I needed out.

In February of 1964, I joined the Navy. I wanted to see the world, to be part of something bigger than myself. My first assignment was aboard the USS Mauna Kea AE22, which was an ammunition ship.

That's where I learned the rhythm of ship life, the clang of steel, the hum of engines, the endless horizon. It was on that ship that I learned how to work with my hands, how to keep calm when things went sideways, and how to trust the man next to you.

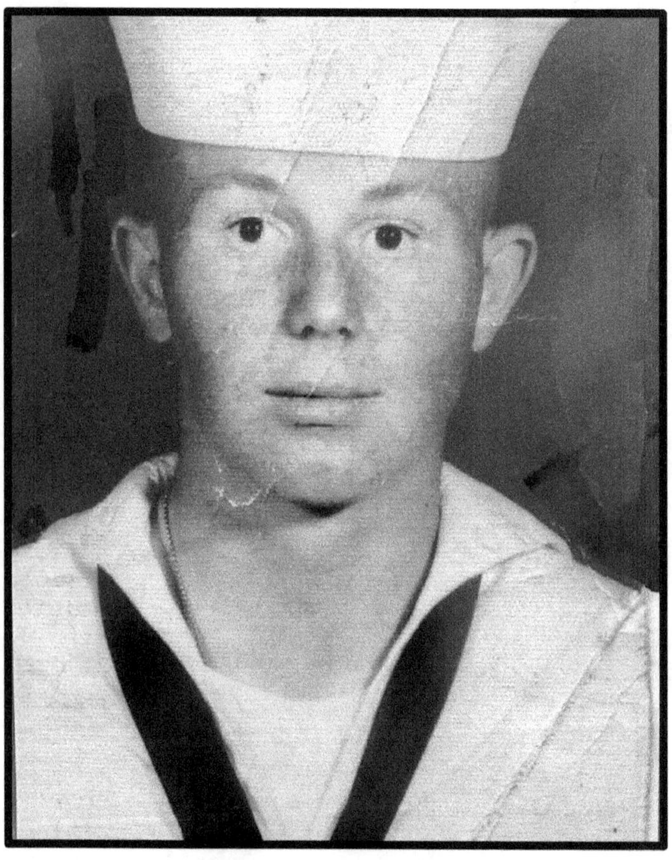

That's me, in Boot Camp, February 1964.

I had no idea then how valuable those lessons would be, or how much I'd come to lean on them. Those lessons would follow me to the *Liberty*. But I can't say those guys felt like brothers. That kind of bond, the kind that comes only when life and death share the same deck, would come later, on the *Liberty*.

I was aboard the Mauna Kea for about eighteen months. I was happy, life was good. My oldest brother, Wayne, was also on the ship. Even though Wayne was my brother, he was a different dude. When we were kids, he'd make me hold up playing cards while he shot at them with his .22. Thank God he was a good shot, but Wayne was different.

Wayne was discharged when his time of service was up, but I stayed on for one more cruise. That second cruise, without Wayne, was when I really felt in charge of my own life. After being out at sea for another six months, we finally made our way back to Port Chicago, in California. It's near San Francisco, and I still don't really know why they called it Port Chicago when it was in California near San Francisco. But heck, I guess that's California for you!

Wayne met me at Port Chicago, and this is where I lost that feeling of being in charge of my life again, because of fucking Wayne. Wayne was homeless at that time; I came to find out. He convinced me to help him sneak on the ship so he had a place to stay, and I did. He slept on the ship with me for two nights, but I couldn't risk it anymore because if they found out, we both would've been court-martialed or worse. Then Wayne convinced me to go AWOL, 'absent without leave', and so we got off the ship.

After getting off the ship, we started hitchhiking to Colorado to go home. Back then, it was easy to hitchhike, especially if you had a uniform on. Being in the military meant something back then, and carried with it respect from civilians. We'd get picked up by random folks who'd drive us for a few hundred miles, then drop us off when they needed to exit Interstate 70. Nothing crazy happened, except for the occasional jackasses who'd pull over slightly ahead of us, and then when we were a few feet away, they'd peel out and leave us in a dust cloud. At the time, I was so pissed, but now I look back and laugh.

We made it back to Colorado, and now I was three days AWOL, which is not good. On day four, we met up with some guys we knew, out at night, driving around being idiots. My buddy Jimmy Jones was driving when we saw sirens and the police. Instead of pulling over, Jimmy sped up, and we were in a high-speed chase going down alleyways and streets. I told him to just pull it over, and let's get out, it's every man for himself. He did. I was AWOL, and now probably getting arrested. We all jumped out of the car, except my younger brother Al, who stayed. Al was actually a great guy, the opposite of Wayne.

Jimmy and I ran and climbed up a tree, and stayed there for at least two hours. I have no idea where Wayne went. Around 4:30 a.m., Jimmy and I got out of the tree and made our way into a backyard. We thought we were in the clear, but damn, we were wrong. The cops came out of nowhere and grabbed us.

I was done. I just lay on the ground with my hands up. They got within four or five feet with their guns drawn, and this was the Denver Police, who at the time had a reputation worse than dog shit. Next thing I know, they sicced their dog, King, on me. I remember his name and his bite clearly, as he took hold of my left leg and shook it like a rag doll. He started coming for my head, and I put my arm over my throat, and the damn dog bit my arm. They got him off me, then arrested us and said we were shooting at the cops. We never even had a gun, but that was the way cops in Denver were back then.

We got arrested and taken down to the station. They had Al, but Wayne was still out there. At the station, Al stood up and pleaded for them to get me a doctor because I was bleeding from King's bite. I remember the cop standing up, putting on his black gloves, and then telling Al to 'sit the fuck down before he knocks the shit out of us.' They let Al go because he had stayed in the car.

I got sent to Denver County Jail for three days, and finally got out of jail because my sister Lori hired an attorney and filed a complaint with the FBI against the Denver Police. The FBI found out that we never had a gun, and so all charges were immediately dropped.

Because I was AWOL now for five days, the cops took me straight to Lowry Air Force Base right outside of Denver. I ended up being in their jail for about a week. The jail for the Air Force was like a hotel compared to the one in Denver. This place was the Hyatt. Then I was transferred to Waukegan, Illinois. That's where they had a red line brig. A brig is another word for jail, and a red line brig is the toughest one you could be assigned to.

I was waiting for a special court-martial, the Navy's version of a criminal trial. The day of my trial in front of my peers, I told them how I regretted my actions and took full responsibility for them, but I begged them not to kick me out of the United States Navy. They sentenced me to thirty days in the red line brig, but they didn't kick me out of the Navy. It felt like a prize, even though I knew how tough the next thirty days would be.

Surprisingly, the brig ended up being easy for me, because I was in there with a bunch of losers who wanted out of the military. For me, staying in the Navy was the most important thing, and so nothing else mattered. The guards even knew it. When my thirty days were up, I'll never forget the guards driving me to the gate and saying, *"Tourney, we never want to see you again, and you never belonged here."* That felt good.

Looking back, I think the brig taught me something I couldn't have learned anywhere else. It showed me who I was when everything was stripped away. No family. No rank. No future guaranteed. Just me, deciding what mattered. And what mattered was staying in. Staying in meant the **Liberty**. And the **Liberty** meant finding the kind of brotherhood that Wayne, God love him, never quite knew how to give me.

After that, my orders came through: I was being reassigned to the **Liberty**. They told me the ship's job was simple: mapping the bottom of the ocean. I didn't know what the hell that meant, but I didn't care. I was just glad to still be in the Navy. I didn't know it then, but that paper and those orders sealed my place in history and would alter the course of my life in ways I never could have imagined.

It was mid-1965 when I got on the ***Liberty***. After that first three months, I realized "mapping the bottom of the ocean" was code for something else entirely. I was aboard a spy ship.

What came next would change everything.

June 8, 1967.

That's the day when the men I'd gotten to know, and even the quiet, secretive ones from the "mapping crew," became my brothers in an instant. After the first attack runs, when the deck was chaos and splinters, I caught sight of Terry Halbardier crawling past me, face black with soot, one arm wrapped around a coil of coax like it was his lifeline. He looked up, grinned, and kept going. He didn't shout for cover; he didn't have to. I leaned out, waited for the next dive, and when the engines peaked, I shoved him forward, then followed.

Near the fo'c'sle, the front of the ship, I saw a sailor carrying a man twice his size, boots dragging through blood and seawater, leaving a dark trail behind them. I ran toward him to help take some of the weight, but he shook his head, jaw locked, eyes empty but steady. "I've got him," he said, like it was a promise to God himself.

Then the jets came again, screaming low, peppering the deck with fire and metal. We threw ourselves over the wounded man, using *our* bodies to provide *him* cover. I felt a shard of hot steel bite into my forearm, but didn't move. He didn't either. When the roar faded, the sailor stood, shoulders trembling, and kept walking, still carrying the man as if the weight didn't matter.

Down below, my friend Rick Aimetti and I worked on the holes that were flooding compartments. We were scared shitless, but there was no time for fear, only work. Rick was steady, hands sure, voice low, like a man fixing a kitchen sink instead of one holding back the sea. We passed wrenches and wedges in silence, listening to the ship breathe. The wedges were just blocks of wood, hammered into ruptured pipes to slow the water. The hull, which is just the steel skin of the ship, kept popping as the **Liberty** settled. Every time the hull popped, we looked at each other. Then we went back to work.

His eyes said, "Again?" Mine answered, "Yeah."

Chief Radioman Wayne Smith kept going where few would, near sparks, near fire, near everything that wanted to kill him, working to repair and reestablish communications under fire. He was trying to coax another circuit back to life, desperate to get a signal out. I watched him kneel beside a wounded sailor, tuck a rag under his head with one hand, and key the transmitter with the other. That gentle, that stubborn, and that brave.

And Captain McGonagle, leg now wide open, stood like a fixed point on the bridge, refusing to move. Blood ran down his leg, pooling at his shoe, but his voice cut clean through the chaos. He didn't shout. He measured. "You. There. Now." A man can be in pain and still lend his spine to everyone around him. That day, his backbone became ours.

We passed canteens to keep men conscious. A sip, a pause, another sip. Just enough to keep them with us. We tore shirts into bandages. We argued over who would carry whom, not because it mattered, but because everyone wanted to help. We tied a lot of tourniquets. When a man shook too hard to tie a tourniquet, the next man took his hands, steadying, knotting, tightening, until the bleeding slowed. If a flashlight died, someone put their body between the flame and the wind, cupped their hands, and kept the light alive.

Some moments stay with you, no matter how many years pass. Francis Brown on the helm, twenty years old and refusing to flinch. Steve Toth's helmet, smoking on the deck where he should've been standing. Allen Blue's face. Duane Hodges's face. Jack Raper's face. Edward Rehmeyer's face. Marines who stood their ground. Names I say under my breath sometimes, like a prayer I don't know all the words to.

When the first torpedo hit, the sound was deafening and the lights went out. Seawater poured in fast. I saw a sailor about my age trying to hold a patch over a ruptured pipe with both hands. The pressure kept forcing him back, but he kept pressing it down. I got beside him, covered his hands with mine, and together we held the patch until the water slowed.

"Don't let go," he said. "I won't."

A corpsman's hands trembled, but he still managed to wrap a bandage. Another sailor quietly whispered Psalms as he cut away burned cloth. Another one, face covered in soot, said he didn't believe in God but held the flashlight steady for the man who did. Faith that night was universal.

After midnight, a small group of us gathered near the torpedo hole. No one planned it; it just happened. Four of us, then six, shoulders touching, heads low. We didn't pray or speak fancy words; we just stood there, breathing the same smoky air. One of the guys, maybe Rick, maybe me, said, "We're still here." Another nodded. We were all thinking the same thing: we were lucky to be alive, but the night wasn't over. There was still work to do if we wanted to stay that way.

In the morning, when the rescue ships showed up, and the questions started, we answered the way we had survived, together. Not because we rehearsed it, but because the truth lived in all of us the same way. We weren't hiding; we were holding. We were making sure no one shouldered more than he already had to.

Brotherhood isn't medals or speeches. It's the small things done without thinking: a canteen lifted to a mouth gently; a body laid over another body; a joke muttered at the wrong time because someone needs to breathe; a name spoken softly because someone needs to be remembered. It's keeping your post when your legs want to quit. It's crawling with coax in your arms because someone has to send the call. It's telling a man the truth when he asks if he's going to make it, and staying there when he doesn't.

People call us brave. People call me brave.

I don't feel brave.

I feel carried. Carried by men whose faces I can still see when I shut my eyes. Men who lent me their steadiness when mine ran out, who handed me their courage like a wrench, so I can use it, and then pass it on. Years later, when my life started to come apart, my marriage breaking down, the drinking getting heavier, I learned that lesson of brotherhood again, only this time without uniforms or rank. A friend answering the phone in the middle of the night. A man at a meeting slides a cup of coffee across the table and says, "Sit." My sons, Bryce and Shane, are quiet but present, sitting beside me.

I used to think surviving meant doing it all on your own, white-knuckling it, and pushing through. That sounds tough, but it's not the truth. The truth is, we get through because of each other. Out there on the **Liberty**, and in all the years after, I didn't make it forward alone. Every step had someone else's fingerprints on it. That's when you feel real humility, knowing your strength was never just yours.

When I speak to young sailors or kids who've never seen the ocean, I tell them this: Courage isn't loud. It's not pretty. It's not even always clean. It's the quiet exchange between people who decide, without fuss, to carry what they can for as long as it takes. It's the hand you don't shake off. It's the voice that says, "Again," and you say, "Okay," and you both move.

We like stories with heroes and endings that make sense. The **Liberty** doesn't give you that. What it gives you is names and faces and moments where men turned toward each other when everything else was turning to ash. That's enough for me.

I didn't survive that day by myself. None of us did.

If I'm still afloat, it's because dozens of hands kept me from going under, on that deck, in that water, and for decades after. And if you want to know what brotherhood is, it's this: I can still feel those hands.

My Reflection...

When I close my eyes, I still see Rick's face in the dark. His eyes said, "Again?" and mine answered, "Yeah." That's all brotherhood ever really was. Showing up one more time when everything in you wants to stop.

We were just kids trying to do a man's job in a world that made no sense. Brotherhood was what kept us steady. It kept us alive and gave us something to hold on to. The fire burned the ship, but it also welded us together in a way only tragedy can.

When I speak of those men now, it's not just out of memory, it's out of gratitude. They taught me what real strength looks like: not muscle or medals, but the simple act of showing up when someone else needs you. They taught me that love doesn't always announce itself; sometimes it sounds like, "You good?" or "Hang on."

No monument can capture what happened on that ship, no ceremony can name every moment of courage. But I carry those moments with me, the hands, the voices, the quiet acts that made survival possible.

If I have one lesson to pass on, it's this: no matter how dark the fire, brotherhood is what keeps the light alive. It's what keeps a person afloat.

Chapter 4: The Weight of Silence

The *Liberty* left the attack site on June 9, 1967, a day after we were hit. They could've sent us to Crete, which was much closer, but instead we were ordered to Malta, the farthest option. Why? To this day, I still wonder if it mattered to someone whether we made it or not.

We had a 40-foot-by-40-foot hole torn through our side, and every sailor on board knew we were one bad wave away from going under. The bulkheads were like balloons, bulged out from the blast of that damn torpedo, and we had to shore them up with whatever we could find to keep them from giving way.

Later that morning, nine of the bodies had been taken off and loaded onto the USS America. The other 25 were sealed inside the wreckage, trapped behind twisted steel and water we couldn't reach. I remember the Communication Technicians, the ones we called "spooks" or "CT's." They were the only men allowed anywhere near where the 25 dead brothers were sealed in the bulkhead. They were the intelligence guys on board, but I'll say this, they worked harder than anyone.

Before the attack, we thought those guys were on another team, and truthfully, we didn't even know what team that was. After the attack, though, all that changed. They were us, and we were them. Every man on board became part of one crew. That has carried on for life with those who made it.

I remember at one point, the 'Old Man', as we called him, Captain McGonagle, told us to hose down what we could and make her look as clean as we could. I remember thinking, who cares how dirty the ship is? But what he wanted us to wash wasn't just the decks; it was the blood and body parts of our brothers. I turned the hose on the steel and blasted my friends' remains into the sea. It was so hot that day, and the blood on the deck was baked in so deep that even with what we called a suicide nozzle, a fitting that gave the hose tremendous pressure, it still wouldn't come clean. I have lived with that memory; it's dark.

Those seven days to get to Malta felt endless. We rotated sleep in two-hour shifts, hands raw from the pumps, clothes soaked with salt and oil. Every few hours, the pumps would sputter, and hearts would stop until they caught again. The engineers worked around the clock, patching leaks with anything they could find: wood, rags, even shirts. Meals were cold and quick; no one had the stomach for much. When the sea got rough, we braced for the worst. I remember staring at the horizon, wondering if I'd ever see land again. For seven long days, our job was simple: keep her alive. We pumped water, patched steel, and prayed that the next hour wouldn't be our last.

By the time the **Liberty** limped into Malta, barely moving, we were spent. I remember it was so sunny. It was peaceful. The world around us was alive, while the **Liberty** looked dead, silent, battered, and bleeding.

From a distance, we could've been any ship returning home from a long patrol. Up close, we were a corpse of a vessel, holes torn through the steel, paint scorched and curling, a gap in her side where the torpedo had ripped us open. We didn't look victorious or even lucky. We looked like what we were: survivors dragging home a dead ship.

When we tied up, I remember seeing the dockworkers frozen where they stood. You could see the shock hit them, mouths half open, tools slipping from their hands. The officers on the pier didn't look much different. Their faces stayed tight, but their eyes said it all. They couldn't believe anyone on that ship was still alive, including the ship herself. The *Liberty* looked like death drifting into a world that had forgotten what war looked like.

I remember thinking, do they know the truth as to what really happened?

That afternoon, they called us into the ship's meeting room for briefings. The room smelled like paper and sweat. An officer read from a sheet, his voice flat and careful. He thanked us for our service, said there would be questions, and told us not to speak about what happened. Not to the press. Not to family. Not to anyone. National security, he said. "Loose talk can cost lives." It was the first time I realized the danger wasn't over; it had just changed from torpedoes to words.

We were questioned one by one. Small rooms, bad lighting, a tape recorder between us. *Where were you when the first rockets hit? What did you see?* I told the truth until I said the word "Israel." Then the officer looked up, cleared his throat, and told me to stick to times and positions. Someone in the corner said, "Let the record show the witness is unsure." But I was not unsure. That's when I felt the shift. That's when I understood this wasn't about finding truth. It was about shaping it.

That night, lying in my bunk, I stared at the ceiling and tried to make sense of what had happened. My country, the one I believed in enough to serve, was asking me to forget. I didn't know yet if I was angry or ashamed. Maybe both. I remember thinking about Mickey LeMay, one of my best friends to this day. He had over a hundred pieces of shrapnel in him, and I still don't know how he survived. What's crazy is, he still has more than eighty pieces in him today. I guess you could call them souvenirs. The idea that my own government would hide what happened to us felt impossible. But it was there, in the way the officers avoided making eye contact and the way they kept correcting us with words like "mistake," trying to put them into our mouths. That word "mistake" burned worse than the napalm. Well, not really, but the pain has lasted longer. It has lasted a lifetime.

For some reason, I kept going back to June 11, just a few days earlier. That's when those two inquiry officers, Admiral Isaac Kidd and Captain Ward Boston, a JAG officer, came aboard with their pressed uniforms, polished shoes, and the whole official look. At the time, their questions made no sense to me. Too careful, too rehearsed, like they were reading from a playbook. I didn't get it then, but looking back now, I do. The questions weren't meant to find the truth; they were meant to box it in. We just didn't realize the script had already been written, and we were only there to say our lines. They took notes, nodded like they were listening, but I know now they already had written their report before they stepped on deck.

To drive that point even further, I remember Admiral Kidd addressing a small group of us in sick bay. He took off his stars and threw them on the table, saying, "I'm just like your dad. Tell me everything." So, I did. I asked him, "Why didn't you guys come and help?" That's when he put his stars back on, and his whole demeanor changed. He stepped in close, right in my face.

"Tourney," he said, "don't ever ask that again, or you'll end up in Leavenworth. Or worse."

He leaned even closer. "Do you know what *worse* means, Tourney?" I did. "Yes, sir."

I was twenty years old, and it rattled me. Looking back now, that moment planted something in me, a deep distrust of authority, or at least of what I was told counted as authority.

When it was all said and done, they basically told us this: Forget it ever happened, and move on with your lives.

After all the interrogations finished, we finally got shore leave. Malta was normal, but we were no longer normal. People went about their day, children ran through the streets, cafés were full. I sat with a few of the guys at a bar. The bartender kept his distance. Every so often, a plane passed overhead, and we'd all go quiet until the sound faded. We never talked about the attack. We didn't have to. The silence said it all.

A week in, I started to see things differently. The gratitude from command didn't feel like honor; it felt like guilt. The flags they raised, the handshakes, the hollow words about bravery, it was all surface. The real story was getting buried. I began to realize that silence wasn't about protecting secrets, it was about protecting people in power. LBJ. McNamara. The men whose decisions had left us to die were now deciding what version of events the world would get to hear.

At night, I'd lie awake replaying the attack. The sounds, the faces, the smell of burning flesh. I kept asking the same question: *Why would they do it?* Why would our allies attack us? Why would our President call back help? And why were we now being told to keep quiet? Each time I thought about it, the anger grew a little heavier. Not rage, just the weight of betrayal setting in slowly.

During those thirty or so days in Malta, we all felt lost. After seven straight days of fighting to stay alive, the sudden stillness was strange. There wasn't enough work to keep us busy the way we had been, so they gave us what they called a 'Free Pass' to go into town and do what we wanted. Maybe it was their way of trying to make us feel normal again, like nothing had happened. So, we went out to the bars along what we called Scum Alley, you can guess why. There weren't any obvious ladies of the night, but if you wanted one, it wasn't hard to find.

I remember hanging out with George Golden, whom we called the Smoky Mountain Jew. I have no idea why, because he was a Baptist. George never seemed to mind it. That was just how we were with each other back then. He was a good guy, and one of the few who could make me laugh during those long days when laughter didn't come easily. One night, a few of us were sitting in a bar talking about the ***Liberty***, just sailors being sailors, trying to make sense of it all, when a man we didn't know came over and told us, "You guys shouldn't be talking about this." We froze. What the hell? Were they following us? Listening in? I still don't know who he was, or who he answered to, but it felt like eyes were on us everywhere we went.

When we finally left Malta, the ***Liberty*** looked better, but we felt worse. Fresh paint. New flags. From a distance, maybe even proud again. But underneath, she was scarred in ways you couldn't see. So were we. We were told we'd done our duty, that the investigation would handle the rest. But I'd already learned what "handle" really meant: file it, stamp it, seal it. Forget about it.

There was something else that didn't sit right with me. When we left Malta, most of us just wanted that torpedo hole patched enough to get us home without sinking. Instead, they went to work like they were remodeling a house, fresh paint, new metal, and polish on every corner. It felt like they were trying to make it look like nothing had happened. We wanted America to see what our so-called greatest ally had done to us, or tried to do to us, but now they were slapping lipstick on a pig. All the cannon and rocket holes that were evidence of wrongdoing, the welders cut them out with a torch and replaced them with flat metal welded over the outside, sealing away the proof. The **Liberty** didn't need to be dressed up; she needed to stand as proof of what really happened. The problem was that they did not want anyone to know what really happened. How crazy is it that the same sentiment has carried on to this day?

We were finally back at sea, headed for our home port in Norfolk, Virginia. There was only a skeleton crew on board, just enough men to bring her home. We ended up doing jobs we'd never done before, covering each other's roles, but I guess that was par for the course after all that had happened.

Then, instead of taking us into Norfolk as expected, they quietly brought us into Little Creek, a smaller naval facility nearby, away from public view. It felt deliberate, like they wanted as few people as possible to even know we were back.

Seriously, what was going on?

The whole thing didn't sit right with me. When we pulled in, there were people there, but nothing near how many should have been had they had known what really happened.

Coming home didn't fix anything. If anything, it made the silence louder. The first few weeks were a blur of well-meaning faces. Family, friends, neighbors, all asking the same questions I couldn't answer. "What happened out there?" I'd open my mouth, then close it.

The truth felt dangerous, like it could get me court-martialed or worse. So, I just said what they wanted to hear: that it was over, that I was lucky to be alive. Lucky never felt like the right word.

Sleep was another battle. I'd wake to the sound of nothing and think it was gunfire. Planes overhead made me flinch. The smell of gasoline would twist my stomach. I tried to drown the memories in whiskey, but all that did was make them louder the next morning. You can't drink your way out of what's true. You can only hide from it for a while.

The Navy sent a letter. Fake condolences. It also had another page that said we'd be compensated $250 for the clothes that were ruined on June 8th, but in return, we'd have to sign something agreeing never to sue the United States Government or the Government of the State of Israel, since this was being called a "case of mistaken identity." Mistaken identity. $250.

I signed the letter. I needed the money. I folded it, put it in a drawer, and never looked at it again. That same week, I went to church for the first time since before the *Liberty*. I didn't ask God for answers. I just sat there. A woman shook my hand and said she'd pray for me. I nodded. She didn't know what for, and I didn't know how to tell her what she actually should be praying for.

Every day that first month felt like walking with a shadow I couldn't shake. I'd go out for groceries, and a car backfiring would take me right back to the deck. I'd be mid-conversation and realize I hadn't heard a word the other person said. The world had moved on, but part of me was still in the Mediterranean, standing over friends I couldn't save. That's what silence does: it traps you in the moment you're trying to escape.

The cover story made the papers not long after: "Mistaken Identity." I read it sitting at the kitchen table, and I laughed, an empty kind of laugh that made my chest hurt. I remember thinking, *if that's the truth they're selling, the world's buying a lie.*

That first story, we made the cover. The next day, the blurb they added was buried in the middle section of the paper. By the third day, there was one last story full of more nonsense, tucked on the back page. The cover-up was complete in three days: front, middle, back. I tore the articles out and kept them. Not as proof for anyone else, but as a reminder to myself: this is how the truth starts to die if you let it.

In the months that followed, I told the story when I could, quietly, to anyone who would listen, but it always felt like shouting into the wind. Some people nodded, some didn't believe a word of it. I learned quickly that truth can make people uncomfortable. So, I stopped trying to make them see. I didn't stop speaking about it altogether, but I stopped expecting anyone to care.

It would take many years before I spoke about it openly, and even longer before the world began to listen. Looking back, I see now that those first few years after the *Liberty* weren't silent; they were the years when I tried to live with the noise still inside me. The hard part wasn't holding my tongue; it was learning how to live with what I couldn't forget. You can survive the attack, survive the fire, even survive the guilt, but learning how to live with the noise that never leaves you? That's the longest war of all.

My Reflection...

I've had a long time to think about silence. Not just the silence they ordered us to keep, but the kind that settles in afterward. The kind that follows you home, shows up at night, and reminds you that some things don't end when the shooting stops.

For years, I told myself staying quiet was part of the job. I was young. I trusted the men above me. I believed that if the truth really mattered, someone else would handle it, someone with rank, someone with authority. What I didn't understand then was that silence doesn't just protect secrets. It protects power. And the longer you carry it, the heavier it gets.

I survived the attack on the *Liberty*. A lot of better men didn't. I survived the fire, the flooding, the days at sea, and the orders to forget. What I didn't survive cleanly was what came after: the confusion, the anger, the knowledge that something deeply wrong had been done and quietly sealed away.

I tried to live a normal life. I worked. I raised a family. I kept my head down. But the truth has a way of resurfacing no matter how deep it's buried. It shows up in your sleep, in your temper, in the way you hear speeches about honor.

I don't tell this story because I enjoy reliving it. I tell it because the 34 men we lost deserve more than a footnote and a cover story. They deserve to be remembered honestly. They deserve to be named. And they deserve a country willing to look at what really happened, even when it's uncomfortable. At my age, I don't care about outrage. I care about truth, the kind that doesn't bend for politics or alliances.

If the *Liberty* taught me anything, it's that surviving doesn't end your responsibility. It begins it.

I lived when others didn't, and I don't pretend to have a clean answer to why. But I do know this:

telling the truth is part of what I owe them. That's why I'm still speaking.

And that's why silence, for me, was not an option.

Chapter 5: The Last Tour

I got out of the Navy on December 12, 1967, hopped into my '66 Ford Galaxy 500, and headed back to Mount Airy, North Carolina. I loved that car. I'd been married two years by then, with a little girl named Frankie. Coming home felt strange, like the world had kept moving while I was stuck somewhere else. I picked up odd jobs here and there, nothing steady. Eventually, I started climbing poles for Floyd Pike Electric, me, a lineman again, working hard and keeping my head down. It wasn't glamorous, but it was work, and it kept food on the table.

I tried to bury the **Liberty** and that day in the Mediterranean. I did it the way a lot of guys did, at the bottom of a bottle. After work, it was the bar. The bar didn't ask questions. It didn't want explanations. It didn't care about June 8th. I felt like nothing could touch me anymore, like I was bulletproof, but at the same time, I felt lost, like I didn't know where I fit in. On nights I didn't go out, I drank at home, same silence. Just lonelier.

Even though I was trying to bury June 8th and everything that happened on board the **Liberty** to the outside world, it still lived inside my head. I just didn't talk about it anymore. I tried, at first. I told people what happened, what we went through, but no one seemed to care. Worse, most didn't believe me. The story about it being a 'mistaken identity' had already been accepted as the truth, and the world had moved on. There wasn't any room left for another version. There wasn't social media back then, or any real way for me to get my story out there, to get the truth out there. I stopped. I kept it inside. That's when I started dying, from the inside out.

One job led to another. I started working in a gambling joint that served hot dogs and cheap whiskey. They ran a poker game in the back, and one night a guy lost big and started shooting the place up. Those gunshots cracked open everything I'd tried to keep down. They didn't sound like North Carolina. They sounded like the Mediterranean, the **Liberty**, the screams, the chaos; it all came roaring back.

I ran out the back door without thinking. Didn't even know I was running until I was in the dark. I still had to go back the next night. Bills don't care about trauma. I had to keep working there because I needed to make ends meet. I guess this was the beginning of staying afloat.

After surviving June 8th, I felt invincible some days. Other days, I felt like I didn't deserve to have made it out. I was 21, angry half the time, and I didn't know what I was even angry about. I gambled a lot. I drank a lot. Shirlene and I argued a lot. Most of that was on me. Looking back, I can see it more clearly. Back then, I just thought that was life. I thought I shouldn't have made it out alive when so many others didn't. In hindsight, none of that should've been an excuse, but I was 21. Who the hell knows.

A decade rolled by. Frankie grew, and we got pregnant again with August Marie. We moved back to Colorado to be closer to family, thinking that would fix us. For a while, it helped. Shirlene and my mom got along. But that didn't last either. We bounced again, this time to California. That fell apart, too, so we ended up right back in North Carolina. We kept thinking a new zip code might fix what was breaking inside us. It didn't.

We both knew something had changed. Love had thinned out. But we stayed together anyway. Maybe for the kids. Maybe out of habit. Maybe because neither of us knew how to start over.

By then, I was lost again, just as when I was thirteen, working for my Dad and trying to figure out what came next. So, I did what I'd done before. I went back to the Navy. Not because I wanted to. Because I had to. I needed to feed my family and keep health insurance.

That was the truth of it. Looking back, it was another version of staying afloat, doing what I had to do to keep my head above water and make sure my family was taken care of. It was survival mode, plain and simple.

They assigned me to the USS *Maddox DD731*, a Gearing-class destroyer built during World War II that saw service throughout the Pacific before becoming part of the Cold War fleet. The Maddox had been tied to the Gulf of Tonkin incident in 1964, the event that opened the door to deeper involvement in Vietnam. Back then, I was just a kid watching the news. Today, I look at events like the Gulf of Tonkin incident very differently.

Most people today have heard of Vietnam, but not many know the name of the ship that helped light that fuse. It was the USS *Maddox* that Washington pointed to as proof of an 'attack' that never really happened. The Gulf of Tonkin mess is what kicked Vietnam into high gear, and maybe became the playbook for the ***Liberty*** attack and set the stage for what was to follow.

The so-called 'incident' in the Gulf in 1964 happened just nine months after Lyndon B. Johnson took over the presidency, after John F. Kennedy was assassinated. It turned out to be a full-blown false flag, used to justify sending thousands of young men into the jungles of Vietnam.

A false flag is when a government carries out or stages an act of aggression, then blames it on another party to justify retaliation or war. History's full of them, like the Reichstag Fire in 1933 Germany, used by Hitler to seize absolute power, or the sinking of the USS *Maine* in 1898, which pushed America into the Spanish-American War.

Even the U.S. military once drafted a plan called *Operation Northwoods* in 1962, proposing fake terrorist attacks on American soil to drum up public support for a war against Cuba. But JFK didn't fall for it; he rejected the plan outright, refusing to manipulate his own people to start another war. Though it was never carried out, the plan showed how far some were willing to go to manipulate the public and steer policy.

The Tonkin incident followed that same playbook. Reports that didn't add up. Confusion turned into misuse of power. A resolution was passed that gave LBJ broad war powers. What was claimed to be an attack never actually happened. It was a setup, plain and simple.

At the time, I was just a teenager when Kennedy was killed, but decades later, I started seeing things differently. Kennedy had been trying to pull troops out of Vietnam, not send more in. He wanted to make good on the warning his predecessor, Dwight D. Eisenhower, had given during his farewell address, the one where Eisenhower cautioned the nation about the rise of what he called the Military-Industrial Complex.

Eisenhower said:

"In the councils of government, we must guard against the acquisition of unwarranted influence, whether sought or unsought, by the military industrial complex. The potential for the disastrous rise of misplaced power exists and will persist."

I remember watching Ike give that speech on a black-and-white TV. Like the rest of the country, I didn't really know what he meant, but I believed him.

JFK knew what he meant.

But after JFK was killed, that warning was ignored, and America went the other way. And right in the middle of it all was President Lyndon B. Johnson. He took that event and used it to ram through the Gulf of Tonkin Resolution, giving him basically a blank check to wage war without

Congress standing in the way. To me, that marked the moment the presidency started to look more like a puppet show than a position of power. You have to wonder who was really pulling the strings. Johnson might've been the first American president openly steered by forces outside our borders, powerful interests, maybe even a foreign hand. Those were the dots that I connected decades later, and ironically, those are the dots that people are connecting now.

Before all of that started making sense to me, I eventually learned more about the political storm that Kennedy had walked into. In addition to wanting to take the United States out of Vietnam, a move that would have cut deep into the pockets of the Military Industrial Complex that Eisenhower warned us about, Kennedy was also clashing with Israel's Prime Minister, David Ben-Gurion.

The two men were at odds over two main issues: Israel's secret nuclear program at the Dimona facility, which Kennedy wanted to inspect and bring under international oversight, and his insistence that the Israeli lobby in Washington register as a foreign agent. That lobby was the predecessor to what we now know as AIPAC, the American Israel Public Affairs Committee, which has become one of the most powerful lobbying organizations in the United States, known for shaping U.S. foreign policy in favor of Israel.

Kennedy was also at war with the three-letter agencies, namely the CIA and the FBI. After the Bay of Pigs invasion in 1961, when a CIA-backed plan to overthrow Fidel Castro in Cuba collapsed in disaster and left the United States embarrassed on the world stage, Kennedy was furious. Aides later recalled him saying he wanted to "splinter the CIA into a thousand pieces and scatter it to the winds." It wasn't a speech. It was a man realizing he'd been handed a plan that blew up in his face.

Around that same time, Kennedy signed Executive Order 11110, which allowed the Treasury to issue silver-backed currency. Some people later argued that it showed he wanted to shift power away from the Federal Reserve. I don't pretend to be an economist, but I do know this: he was willing to challenge powerful institutions. And when a president starts challenging powerful institutions, he makes powerful enemies.

When Kennedy was assassinated, it was more than just a change in leadership; it felt like a change in direction. Lyndon Johnson didn't just step into the office; he stepped onto a different path. Vietnam escalated fast. What had been advisory support turned into a full-scale commitment. The Gulf of Tonkin Resolution gave Johnson broad authority to wage war without a formal declaration from Congress, and the conflict expanded in a way Kennedy had been publicly cautious about.

While Kennedy had clashed with the CIA after the Bay of Pigs, under Johnson, the Agency's power didn't shrink; it grew. Covert operations continued. The FBI under J. Edgar Hoover remained firmly in place, and domestic surveillance expanded during those years. Whatever tensions had existed between Kennedy and the intelligence community seemed to fade into the background.

On the foreign policy front, whereas Kennedy had pressed Israel's leadership over inspections at the Dimona nuclear facility, after his death, that pressure eased. The issue of forcing the Israeli lobby in Washington to register as a foreign agent also quietly disappeared from the conversation.

I'm not a historian. I'm just a sailor who lived through the consequences. But from where I stood, it looked like the country pivoted. The warning Eisenhower had given about the Military Industrial Complex didn't sound theoretical anymore. It sounded current. And powerful interests, the kind that operate far above enlisted men and deck plates, seemed to tighten their grip.

Maybe that's why one question has stayed with me all these years. It changed the way I see my country. And no one has ever answered it:

Did Lyndon B. Johnson know what was going to happen with the USS *Liberty* and sign off on it?

Or was he being misled, the way they tried with Kennedy and *Operation Northwoods*, only this time, Johnson chose differently?

Sitting there on the *Maddox*, I couldn't help but think that maybe this was the same kind of road map they'd intended to use with the *Liberty*. Stir chaos, control the story, and get the war they wanted. First, the *Maddox* and Vietnam, then the *Liberty* in the Six-Day War. You start to see a pattern after a while. I saw it then. I still see it now. Decisions made far above the men who pay for them.

But unlike Kennedy, who refused to sacrifice Americans for politics, Johnson seemed to protect his so-called greatest ally instead, leaving the American crew aboard AGTR-5 to pay the price. It's a thought that still doesn't sit right with me.

I'd been back in about six months when they lined us up for inspection. I had my medals pinned, the Bronze Star with the "V" for Valor and the Purple Heart for being wounded but staying in the fight. The Executive Officer stopped when he saw me. "How'd you get these, Tourney?" he asked.

"I was on the *Liberty*," I told him.

He shook his head and said, "Nah, that's stolen valor, Tourney. The *Liberty* was a case of mistaken identity."

Right then, I wanted to punch him in the face, but I didn't. My fists were clenched so tight I could feel my nails cutting into my palms. That lineup for inspection hit me harder than any fight ever had.

Lying there that night in my bunk, staring at the ceiling, I decided I was done. It's one thing for some drunk in a bar to call you a liar; hell, I could live with that. I did live with that.

But for my own Executive Officer to humiliate me in front of the crew, to question what I'd bled for, that cut deep. That's not why I joined the

Navy. I joined to serve my country, not to be called a fraud by the very people wearing the same uniform. The next morning, I went to my quarters and put in for an honorable discharge. I didn't yell, didn't make a scene, I just said I wanted out. A week later, the papers were signed. I put on my uniform one last time, walked off the USS *Maddox*, and didn't look back. That was it. I was done for good.

When I was leaving the Quarterdeck, I saluted the ensign, the flag flown at the ship's stern to show a vessel's nationality and honor its service. That was my last salute. This was probably the first time in my life that I stood up for myself, even though I really needed that job. But staying afloat isn't just about getting by; it's also about holding on to your self-respect and integrity. It's about being able to look the man in the mirror in the eye. That chapter of my life was over.

My Reflection...

Walking away that day didn't feel like freedom. It felt like something I had to do, even though it cost me. I'd spent years trying to be a good sailor, a good husband, a good man, and somewhere between the battles overseas and the silence back home, I lost my footing. The Navy gave me purpose once. It also took things from me that I never fully got back.

But stepping off the Maddox felt different. It wasn't anger. It was clarity. It was one thing to serve your country, which I did, and I did it with pride. But it's another thing to serve men who are supposed to be your brothers and watch them treat you like a subordinate, like your sacrifice doesn't mean a damn thing.

On the **Liberty**, those guys were my brothers. We didn't need rank to define us. We bled together. We carried each other. What held us together wasn't policy or politics; it was survival and loyalty.

On the *Maddox*, they were my superiors. They were detached, cold, and by the book. They conducted needless inspections and only wanted official answers. That's when I realized the Navy I had signed up for, or maybe the one I thought I had signed up for, was gone.

When I left that ship, I didn't just leave the military. I left the last part of me that still believed the institution would protect its own.

I left the part of myself that still believed in it.

Chapter 6: Staying Afloat (Again)

I was twenty-three when I walked off the Maddox for the last time. I didn't make a speech. I just left. The Navy chapter was done, and I would never go back.

Shirlene and I were living in North Carolina then. Her old man, Millard, had forty acres of tobacco fields that stretched as far as you could see. He rented us a trailer on the property for a hundred bucks a month, and that was kind of him. I worked the fields with him, priming tobacco. It was sticky work. Your hands turned black. Your clothes turned stiff from the gum. But after years at sea, dirt and sweat felt honest.

It wasn't glamorous, but it was quiet. That alone made it better than life at sea.

The problem was that Shirlene and I couldn't stand each other anymore. We fought about everything. Her parents were mostly on my side, which only made it worse for her. Home wasn't peaceful. So, I drank. Sometimes three or four days straight. I'd disappear. She stopped asking where I went. She didn't care, and in some strange way, that made it easier.

I wasn't happy. I wasn't sad either. I was just there. I didn't stay in touch with anyone from the **Liberty** or the *Maddox*. I didn't want to. That part of my life was sealed off. I didn't need reminders. I just needed the next drink and a quiet place to sit with it.

Then my brother Al called from Denver. He was selling vacuum cleaners, sewing machines, stereos, the whole door-to-door hustle. He told me to come out, said he'd take me under his wing. Al was the steady one in the family, the normal one, so I listened.

We packed up what little we had and went west, again.

Turns out I could sell. I'd spent years reading men in tight spaces. Sailors. Officers. Liars. You learn how to read a room fast when you've lived through what I had. Money started coming in. For the first time in a long while, I felt capable again.

Then Shirlene wanted to move back to North Carolina. I didn't want to go. But I went anyway. That's what I did back then. I reacted. I didn't decide.

Back in North Carolina, I took what I'd learned in Denver and went into business for myself.

Bought up used sewing machines, cleaned them, fixed them, and sold them in the paper. People loved a deal. I started making more money in a week than most people did in a month.

I opened a little shop with a big sign out front that read: **DO YOU WANT TO MAKE MONEY?**

That sign made me laugh every morning. Because, hell, I finally was. I was living the American Dream, my own boss, full pockets, clean conscience.

But money doesn't fix a broken marriage.

Shirlene and I fought harder than ever. Every word out of her mouth felt like a jab. Every silence between us felt like a mile. One day, it just boiled over. She told me she never wanted to see my face again.

And that was that. I left.

I went back to Denver. I left my wife, and I left my kids. I did that, and that's something I still carry. I'm not proud of it. You don't outrun that kind of guilt. You just learn to live with it. I stayed in touch the best I could. I paid my child support. But money doesn't raise children. Being there does.

Shirlene remarried not long after, and oddly enough, that helped. We stopped fighting. She found peace. Maybe I did too, in my own strange way.

Back in Denver, I was single again, and for the first time in years, I could breathe. I was still drinking, but it didn't run me the way it had before. It had stopped being medicine and started being just a habit. I had friends. I laughed more. Real laughs. The kind that catches you off guard.

One night, I was at a bar with my brother-in-law. There was a volleyball game going on outside, people drinking beer, and good music playing. It was one of those warm nights where everything feels better than it really was.

I saw this girl playing volleyball; she was tall, pretty, with a really nice smile. She caught my eye, but that was it. I got drunk, and I went home.

Next night, same bar. She was there again, sitting with her friends. This time, I was alone.

One of her friends waved me over. "Come sit with us," she said. I walked over.

"I'm Phil," I said.

She smiled.

"I'm Lisa."

And just like that, the next chapter of my life began.

My Reflection…

Leaving the Navy was supposed to be freedom, but it wasn't. It was survival.

I thought getting away from the ships, the orders, and the noise would fix me. It didn't. You can't wash off that kind of life with a hot shower and a clean shirt. You carry it with you, in how you talk, in how you fight, in what you run to when you're tired.

For a long time, I was just staying afloat. Not sinking, but not swimming either. That's a hard place to live. You're breathing, but you're not really living.

But sometimes, that's when the healing starts. Healing didn't look brave. It didn't look strong. It looked slow. It looked messy. It looked like mistakes.

I didn't know it then, but meeting Lisa was the beginning of something better. Not because she rescued me.

Because I finally stopped trying to drown what I didn't want to face.

Chapter 7: The Ship That Never Sank

We talked for a while that night at the bar, then I took off. Lisa was going through her own mess, still technically married, separated, figuring her life out. I'd been divorced for five years and wasn't sure I ever wanted to do that whole thing again. But she was different. There was something quiet about her that felt steady.

I gave her my number. A few days later, she called. Our first date was easy. No pretending. She laughed at my rough edges instead of trying to sand them down. She had this roommate, a guy she'd found in the classifieds, and we all hung around a local bar called Whiskey Bill's.

Then one night, a fight broke out. A knife. Blood on the floor. Someone got stabbed and didn't make it. The next day, the cops called Lisa and said it was her roommate, Lesley. He'd done the stabbing. But the call wasn't to question her, it was to tell Lisa that Lesley had killed himself in their apartment.

Turns out, he'd already been in jail once before for stabbing someone. Guess he knew he wasn't going back. Not exactly how you expect things to begin. But we made it through. If you survive something like that right at the start, you start to believe you can survive anything. We moved in together, she finalized her divorce, and soon after, we eloped in Vegas. No big ceremony, just two people trying to rewrite their lives. She became Mrs. Tourney, and for the first time in a long time, I felt like things weren't working against me.

Remember, I already had two kids from my first marriage to Shirlene, Frankie and August. One day, Frankie called, saying she was having trouble at home. She wanted to come live with us. She stayed for three years and graduated from high school under our roof. Lisa didn't just accept her; she welcomed her.

Lisa also made me feel grounded. She made me believe things could be steady. She gave me confidence, peace, and a kind of calm that I hadn't known since before the **Liberty**.

We started a business together. We built a home from the ground up. We built a life, brick by brick, paycheck by paycheck. She was my balance. My anchor. And for a while, I really thought that was enough.

Then one day in late 1984, my mom called. She said there was an article in the Rocky Mountain News written by a man named Stan White.

Stan White wasn't just some reporter; he'd been there. A master chief petty officer aboard the **USS *Liberty***. He'd survived that same hell I did. During the attack, his station was deep in the repair shops below deck, where he watched the ship buckle and the wounded crawl through the smoke. He'd spent the hours after the bombing stepping over bodies, trying to save whoever was still breathing.

After the Navy buried the story, Stan White refused to stay quiet. He became one of the first to speak out publicly about what really happened that day, the attack, the rockets, the torpedoes, the silence that followed. He spoke publicly. He wrote openly. In one article he wrote, 'Torn and mutilated bodies were everywhere.'

He'd written that the 34 men who died on the *Liberty* would be disappointed to know their country still hadn't told the truth. That's what my mom had read in the paper. That hit me like a punch to the chest.

In all the time we'd been together, Lisa didn't know anything about my military life. Not that I'd been in the Navy. Not that I'd been on that ship. When I brought home the article, I handed it to her. As she started reading it, I said quietly, "I was on this ship."

She stared at me, waiting for the punchline. But it wasn't a joke. She believed me instantly. No questions, no judgment. Just belief. That moment opened something I'd kept shut for years. For the first time, I didn't have to carry the secret alone. Lisa didn't just accept it; she encouraged it. She told me to do what I needed to do.

And that's where everything changed.

On St. Patrick's Day 1985, I made a sign that said **Remember the *Liberty*** and went down to join a group of veterans marching in a parade. I asked if I could walk with them, and they said, "Hell yes, get in front." That was the start of something I didn't see coming.

The **USS *Liberty* Veterans Association** had just formed a couple of years earlier. Stan White helped start it. Lisa pushed me to get involved. She typed my letters while I wrote them, late into the night. She said she was proud of me. I think she was, at first.

A few years later, our first child, Deidre, was born. Then Bryce. Then Shane. Three kids in six years. Lisa used to joke that she was either pregnant or nursing for the first decade of our marriage. It was chaos, but the beautiful kind, the kind that feels like family.

But while my kids were growing up, a part of me was drifting. Not away from them because I didn't love them, but because something old had its hooks in me again.

The *Liberty*.

Looking back now, I see how it started small, a few letters, a few phone calls, a few meetings. Then the full weight of the *Liberty* came back into my life. Once I opened that door, it didn't close again. The guilt came back. The survivor's remorse. The faces of the 34 men who never got to build houses, or raise kids, or grow old.

Lisa had brought me peace, but in doing so, she had given me the space to open a wound I had no idea how to close. The *Liberty* was already there; she just didn't know how deep it ran. And she couldn't stop it.

I became obsessed. If I wasn't working, I was writing about the *Liberty*. If I wasn't home, I was traveling for it. *Liberty* first, *Liberty* second, family maybe.

Lisa used to say she lost her husband to a ship that never sank before she ever met him. She wasn't wrong. It was *Liberty* first. *Liberty* second. Family… maybe.

Guilt became part of my daily life. Guilt for surviving. Guilt for loving. Guilt for raising kids when 34 of my brothers never got that chance.

Those men died so young, their ages ranged from nineteen to thirty-nine. They were just getting started. And here I was, drinking coffee in my kitchen, tucking my kids into bed, pretending life was normal. I felt like I owed them something. Like their lives were the reason I was still breathing. So, I started talking. I wrote letters. I marched. I told the truth to anyone who would listen.

But nobody cared. Not the President. Not Congress. Not the media. Not my friends. Not my family. The silence was louder than the bombs that day. After a while, I'm not sure that even Lisa cared the same way anymore.

Maybe that's what drove me. If the world wouldn't remember them, I would. Those 34 men never got the life I did. I wasn't going to let them disappear.

My Reflection…

Lisa gave me more than love. She gave me room to face something I had spent years avoiding.

I thought I was building a life. In some ways, I was. But I was also building my identity around the *Liberty* again. What started as a few letters and meetings slowly became the center of everything.
She stood by me through it, even when I wasn't fully present. That's hard to admit, but I do. I wasn't easy to live with.

I carried anger. The story of the *Liberty* needed to be told. But my kids needed a father. I convinced myself I could do both. Some days I could. Some days the ship won.

I carried guilt. Some days, I carried it into the house with me. I told myself I was fighting for the 34 men who never got to grow old. That was true. But I didn't always see what it was costing the people who were still here.

It took me longer than it should have to understand that. I realized that trying to stay afloat in life isn't just about surviving what tried to kill you. It's about paying attention to the ones still beside you.

Chapter 8: The L.V.A.

When I first joined the Liberty Veterans Association, they gave me the title of Public Relations Officer. It sounded important, but really it meant I wrote letters until my hands cramped. I wrote to Congress, to Senators, to the Pentagon, to anyone who might bother to read past the first line. I put everything I knew into those letters, hoping someone would finally care. At that point in my life, it felt like the only thing I could actually control.

One of my best letters was to Senator Ted Kennedy. I gave him a detailed account of what happened on June 8, 1967, the real version, not the sanitized narrative the press ran with. I told him we weren't dealing with "mistaken identity," and all we wanted was our day in front of Congress. It was honest, sharp, and relentless. I knew I was writing to the same man who drove off a bridge in 1969 and left Mary Jo Kopechne to drown in the car he escaped from, but I sent the letter anyway. The cause was bigger than the man.

Most of my letters went unanswered. I would wait weeks, sometimes months, for a response that rarely came. When something finally did arrive, I'd hold the envelope like it contained my freedom. Then I'd open it and find some generic form letter thanking me for "*my concern*" and promising they were "*looking into it*." That kind of dismissal didn't just frustrate me; it got under my skin in ways I didn't even understand at the time.

But my fellow survivors kept me going. By then, over 120 **Liberty** men were active in the L.V.A., and there was a solidarity that felt real. We traveled to Washington. We held reunions that were equal parts joy and heartbreak. We visited the graves at Arlington, where 6 of our 34 fallen brothers are buried in a single plot, yet it always felt like all of them were standing beside us. Those moments fueled me. They reminded me why I kept fighting. By the way, the mass grave at Arlington is in Section 34. 34.

Then it happened. It finally happened. During the first Gulf War, the White House invited us to the Rose Garden. They said President George H. W. Bush wanted to see us, hear us, and acknowledge what we had endured. It felt like the moment we had been praying for, a chance to finally break the silence that had suffocated us for decades. For the first time in years, hope didn't feel like a trap.

A huge group of us went. The day was so hot, the kind of heat that makes the air feel heavy.

We stood outside for hours, sweating through our clothes. Captain McGonagle stood among us in his full-dress uniform, his Medal of Honor shining on his chest. The credentials on that man alone should have commanded respect. We were tired, but we were ready to speak our truth at last.

After waiting for hours, a limo rolled up. The President sat inside, windows tinted, the world shut out. He rolled the window down, waved at us, and rolled it back up. Then the car floated past and disappeared. That was it.

Disappointment I could have handled. That felt like we didn't matter. That was the moment I felt something inside me shift.

A few minutes later, Lieutenant General Brent Scowcroft and Chief of Staff John Sununu came out to meet us. They told us the President had *"urgent national security matters"* and wouldn't be joining us after all. Instead, we were being offered a tour of the White House. A tour. That's what we were offered, as if we were school kids on a field trip. After everything we'd carried, that was all they thought we deserved.

I couldn't stomach it. Neither could Lisa.

We didn't go inside. The other men tried to make the best of it, but I could see the pain in their eyes. That day reopened wounds I thought I'd buried, and the betrayal cut deeper than I expected. That's when I understood Washington wasn't coming to help us. They were never going to fight for us. They barely wanted to admit we existed.

After that, I threw myself into the cause with a fury I couldn't explain. If I wasn't at work, I was writing letters. If I wasn't writing letters, I was traveling to speak about the **Liberty**. When I was home, my mind wasn't there. Before I knew it, the **Liberty** was back at the center of my life. Lisa felt it long before I did, and she had said it herself: she lost her husband to a ship that never sank before she ever met him.

At the time, I brushed it off, telling myself she didn't understand. But she understood perfectly. She saw how the guilt had rewired me, how the ghosts of the **Liberty** followed me into every room, every conversation, every quiet moment. She loved me, but she also watched me disappear.

The truth is, the guilt had never left. I still felt guilty for being alive, guilty for moving on, guilty for raising kids when so many of my brothers never got the chance. The government's refusal to acknowledge the truth only made it worse. If they wouldn't fight for those 34 men, then I felt I had to. The weight of that responsibility nearly crushed me, but it also kept me going.

Somewhere in the middle of all that anger and exhaustion, I started reaching for something I had ignored most of my life. It wasn't dramatic. I didn't fall to my knees. I just started talking, quietly, asking for strength, for direction, for some kind of peace.

At first, it felt like I was talking to myself. Over time, it didn't feel that way anymore. Faith didn't erase the guilt. It didn't fix Washington. It didn't bring the 34 men back. But it steadied me. It gave me something that didn't depend on hearings or headlines. It gave me breath when I felt tight in the chest.

Faith was the first thing in a long time that didn't leave me.

My Reflection…

I didn't come to faith because I had it all figured out. I came to it because I was worn out. The guilt, the anger, the silence from Washington, it all piled up. I couldn't carry it by myself anymore.

Faith didn't erase what happened. It didn't ease the painful memories. It didn't answer the questions that had followed me since June 8, 1967. Why did they do it? Why did our own government let it happen? Why did 34 men die and the world just move on? Those questions didn't go away.

But faith gave me somewhere to put them when I couldn't hold them anymore. It gave me somewhere to turn when the weight felt too heavy.

I used to think being strong meant handling everything alone. White-knuckling it. Pushing through. I'd done that for decades, and it nearly destroyed me. I learned that real strength sometimes looks like admitting you can't do it by yourself. That asking for help isn't a weakness. That laying something down doesn't mean you've given up the fight.

Faith didn't change me overnight. But it steadied me. It gave me something Washington never could. Something that didn't depend on hearings or headlines or whether the right people finally decided to care. It was just there. Quiet and steady. Like Lisa. Like the men on that deck who showed up for each other without being asked.

The next thirty years would test that steadiness in ways I couldn't have predicted. But for the first time in a long time, I felt like I had something solid underneath me.

And I was going to need it.

Chapter 9: In the Shadow of the *Liberty*

For most of this book, you've heard my voice. But there's another side to this story.

The **USS *Liberty*** didn't just affect the men who were on that ship. It affected the people who lived with us after.

I asked my children to tell me what it was like growing up with me, with the *Liberty* always in the room. Some agreed to speak. Some chose not to. I respect both.

This chapter belongs to them.

Frankie...

My Dad has been a positive person in my life, and I want to start there. I don't want anyone reading this to think poorly of him. He's still my Dad, and I love him. But if we're going to tell the truth, we need to tell all of it.

My parents were very young when they married. My mom was seventeen when she got pregnant with me and turned eighteen the day after I was born. My Dad was only a year or two older. He was handsome, charismatic, confident, the kind of man who carried himself like he had everything under control, even if he didn't. My grandmother adored him, and my mom fell hard.

Some of my earliest memories are vivid and unsettling. I remember hiding behind curtains in a small apartment in California. I remember yelling and volatility. I remember crying. Years later, my mom confirmed that the memories were real. That was the environment I first understood as "normal."

But I also remember stability. I remember being sent back to North Carolina to live with my grandparents because my parents were too young and overwhelmed to manage everything. My grandfather sold livestock to buy my mom a bus ticket. She had almost nothing, and a stranger on the Greyhound bus bought me diapers because she couldn't afford them. I stayed with my grandparents for about a year and bonded deeply with them.

My grandmother told me I cried for my mom at night and ran a fever. I was old enough to say "Mommy," but not old enough to understand why she was gone. That separation left something in me. At the same time, my grandparents gave me security and steadiness that shaped me in ways I'm still grateful for.

Then there was the reunion. I remember a green hotel building and my Dad in a white shirt bending down and saying, "Come here, Frankie." I ran straight to him. I always thought my Dad was so handsome and strong. I idolized him.

But even as a little girl, I felt like I had to earn his love. That feeling followed me into adulthood, into my marriage, my divorce, and every relationship I've ever had. I spent much of my life trying to prove I was enough. When you idolize someone but feel uncertain of their approval, that pattern sinks deep.

When I was ten, my sister August was born. I loved her immediately and took care of her like she was my own child. I fed her, bathed her, and put her to sleep. She wouldn't sleep unless I was in the room. When parents aren't stable, siblings step in, and children grow up quickly. I did. She did too.

My Dad liked to move, California, Colorado, back again. There wasn't much consistency. My mom worked constantly, and my Dad struggled with gambling and instability. When I was twelve, my parents divorced. My Dad drove us back to North Carolina, dropped us off, and flew back to Colorado. I didn't see him again for six years.

Six years is a long time for a little girl.

Later, when I was a teenager and needed him, he sent me a plane ticket and told me to come live with him. I wanted my Dad. I wanted that connection back. My grandfather took me to the airport without arguing, even though I knew it hurt him. I lived with my Dad and Lisa for my last two years of high school.

Looking back, I sometimes wonder if bringing me out there was part of the ongoing tension between my parents. Maybe it was about proving something. I don't know. At the time, I didn't care. I was with my Dad again.

Life there wasn't perfect. My Dad and Lisa had their own struggles, and I was a teenager trying to find my place. When they went to Vegas and came back married without telling me beforehand, it hurt more than I admitted. I spiraled for a while after that. I felt unseen again.

As I've gotten older, I feel less anger and more compassion. My parents were kids trying to survive adult problems. My Dad had gone through something at eighteen or nineteen that most people can't imagine. The **USS *Liberty*** wasn't just an event; it was trauma layered with betrayal and silence. I can see now how that would change a person. I can see how something like that, happening so young, would shape a man for the rest of his life.

Understanding that doesn't erase what was hard. It doesn't erase the instability or the absence. But it helps me see him as human. I see a man who loved me but didn't always know how to show it in ways that made me feel secure.

I love my Dad. I see him clearly now, the strengths and the wounds. I see a young man who was broken before he ever had a chance to be a father, and a father who loved me even when he struggled to show it. And I see a little girl who wanted his approval more than anything. Hopefully, I finally have it. Because he has mine.

Deidre (Dee)…

When I think about my Dad, the first thing that comes to mind is simple: he was always there. He was present in our lives. I never questioned whether he loved us or whether he would show up. That part of him was steady. But alongside him, there was something else that was always present, too.

The *Liberty*.

I honestly can't remember a time when I didn't know about it. I don't know exactly how old I was when he first explained everything, but I grew up hearing the story. I understood that he had been on a ship that was attacked. I understood that men died. And I understood that he believed the truth about what happened had been buried.

It wasn't something that was whispered about in our house. It was part of daily life. It was on the phone constantly. It was in letters spread across the kitchen table. It was in conversations with his shipmates. It was in planning reunions and traveling to speak. The **Liberty** wasn't just part of his past. It lived in our home.

There were moments when I thought, "Oh my gosh, enough already." It was constant. But I wouldn't say I was sick of it in a resentful way. It was simply woven into who he was. It almost felt like another family member that never left.

My mom was supportive. Always. I think there were times when it caused tension because it took up so much space in our lives, but she stood by him. She believed in him and in what he was trying to do. Even when it was hard, she didn't dismiss it.

I was a Daddy's girl. My brothers would probably agree with that. I always got along well with him. He was protective, sometimes extremely protective. Maybe even a little paranoid. But it came from wanting to keep us safe.

There is one memory that has never left me.

I was probably six or seven years old. My parents had friends over, and the phone rang. Whoever was on the other end told my Dad that if he didn't stop talking about the **Liberty**, they were going to kill our whole family. They said they would start with me, by name.

I was just a little kid. I remember thinking, "Why me first?" I didn't understand politics or power or threats. I just knew someone had said they were going to kill me. That stays with you.

There were other threats over the years. It wasn't a one-time thing. But that one moment made it real in a different way. It actually showed me that what my Dad was doing mattered to someone powerful enough to try to silence him. And even with that, he didn't stop.

As I've gotten older, especially with everything that's happened recently, I feel proud. My Dad has worked every day of my life trying to get that story out. Every single day. People dismissed him. People ignored him. Some people called him a liar.

Now people are finally listening.

When he went on Candace and told his story, I wasn't surprised at the reaction. He's been preparing for that moment for decades. He deserves the recognition. He's worked harder than anyone knows. And he truly does have one of the biggest hearts.

We used to go to *Liberty* reunions when we were kids, in California, Virginia Beach, wherever they were held. I would watch him speak. I would watch the other men listen. I could see the respect in the room. No one else's Dad had stories like that. No one else's Dad carried something that heavy.

The *Liberty* shaped our family in ways that were complicated. It took up space. It caused tension at times. It brought fear into our house. But it also brought purpose. It gave my Dad something he believed in with his whole heart.

The *Liberty* became part of our family whether we wanted it to or not. It shaped us, tested us, and defined so much of our lives. But when I look at my Dad, I don't see just the fight, I see his heart. And that's what I've always been proud of.

Bryce…

Some of my earliest memories of my Dad are tied to chaos.

We were living in a trailer on fifty acres in Colorado. We were poor, but we had land. I remember him surprising us with bunk beds already set up, like he was trying to build something new. But I also remember the fighting. I remember the drinking. I remember my mom crying and yelling that all he cared about was the *Liberty*.

The *Liberty* was always there, even when I was four or five. It wasn't just a story from the past. It was a presence in our house. It was the reason for long phone calls and my Mom writing all those letters for Dad. It was the reason arguments lasted until midnight, while my sister turned the TV up loud so my brother and I wouldn't hear what was happening downstairs.

When you grow up inside something like that, you don't think it's abnormal. You just think that's what life is.

Some nights blurred together. My parents drunk in the hot tub. My Dad coming inside, furious about something and taking it out on us. I remember being made to stand at attention in the corner while he barked military orders at my brother and me for hours. I was eight or nine years old.

I remember opening my bedroom window once and thinking about jumping out just so I wouldn't have to live like that anymore. I didn't. But I remember what it felt like to want to.

There was another night when he drank too much and mixed it with pills. On the drive home, he collapsed on the floor of the car, eyes open, unresponsive. I thought he was dead. I remember screaming. I remember being dropped off at a relative's house while he was taken to the hospital. The next morning, it was like nothing had happened. We never spoke about it again.

That was the rhythm of our house. Explosions. Silence. Move on.

By middle school, I was already six-foot-four. I looked like a grown man before I felt like one. And I think that mattered. My Dad treated me differently than my brother and sister. He was harder on me. Quicker to anger. More physical. There were times he shoved me, hit me, and kicked me when I was down, figuratively speaking, on that last one.

I resented him for it. All of it.

At some point, I stopped seeing him as a father and started seeing him as an adversary. We didn't like each other. We tolerated each other. The **Liberty**, in my mind, became the root of everything: the drinking, the rage, the obsession, the instability.

So, I shut it off.

I found punk rock music. I found friends. I learned that if I were funny and self-deprecating, people would like me. I built a persona. It was easier to be loud and rebellious than to admit I was scared or confused.

The truth is more complicated than that.

But even when we didn't get along, he showed up. He bought me my first bass guitar. He sanded it down and painted it himself. He drove me to every show and stood in the back of grimy venues watching me play. My Dad didn't know how to say he loved me. So, he bought things. He built things. He showed up.

That duality defined us.

When I was sixteen, it finally came to a head. He grabbed my car keys. I pushed back. We ended up in a full fight in the driveway. Not a scuffle. A real fight. I broke the ribs on his right side. I had him on the ground and could have done real damage.

I didn't.

Later, he told me he knew I could have hurt him worse. That moment shifted something. It wasn't father and son anymore. It was man-to-man.

By my teenage years, I told myself I hated him. I told myself I wanted nothing to do with the **Liberty**. I believed it had ruined our family. I believed it had rewired him into someone volatile and unreachable.

For a long time, that's the story I carried.

Then I joined the Military. Then I went to war.

Years later, after my own deployment, we stood at a ceremony. We saluted. The songs played. They dismissed us to our families. I saw my Dad in the crowd the whole time. I remember thinking, There he is.

When we finally met face to face, I hugged him. And the only thing I could say was, "I get it now. I get it."

Because I did.

What happened to him at eighteen or nineteen years old didn't stay on that ship. It followed him home. It followed him into marriage. It followed him into fatherhood. It followed him into every argument and every silence.

As a kid, I only saw the damage.

As a man, I see the wound.

I understand now how something like that could shape a father long after the battle ended. And like so many others, I am starting to understand who caused it.

Shane…

Some of my first memories of the **USS *Liberty*** aren't dramatic. They're just… there. I remember an old documentary playing when I was young. I remember going to reunions in places like San Diego and Virginia Beach. I was probably six, maybe nine, and I didn't fully understand what any of it meant. I just knew it was important.

At that age, it didn't feel positive or negative. It just was. I was around a lot of older men, listening to stories I couldn't fully process. But I remember the solemn moments, the bell ringing, the names being read, the silence that followed. I remember two Navy SEALs swimming a wreath out into the water during a memorial. Even as a kid, I could feel the gravity of it.

As I got older, I started to realize how little people knew about it. Nobody knew about it. I did a class project on the **USS *Liberty*** in fifth grade, and even my teacher didn't know the story. That stuck with me. How could something this big be something nobody talked about? It was one of the first times I understood that history isn't always told the way it happened.

Like my brother, I also joined the military, and yes, my Dad played a role in that. It wasn't about revenge or exposing the truth. It was more about exposure, hearing his stories about the Navy, the good parts too. I felt called to it. It felt natural.

Ironically, my Dad didn't want me to join. I think what happened to him made him cautious. Maybe even gun-shy. He knew what governments are capable of. He didn't want me to become cannon fodder. But over time, he became proud of it.

Growing up, our house wasn't perfect. There were arguments. There was drinking. There were outbursts. My parents had their dynamic, and it wasn't always healthy, but they loved each other. And they did the best they knew how to do.

Bryce and I had different relationships with Dad. Part of that was personality. Part of that was timing. I saw how hard Dad could be on Bryce, and in some ways, that became a motivator for me. I learned early that if I performed, if I handled my business, my life was smoother. That shaped me.

I don't carry resentment toward my Dad. I see the whole picture. I see a man shaped by trauma at nineteen years old. I see PTSD before anyone was really calling it that. I see a guy who didn't have a manual for being a husband or a father. And I see someone who still showed up.

When he went on bigger platforms and finally started getting attention for the *Liberty*, especially the Candace Owens interview, I felt relief. That's the word. Relief. Like, finally someone was listening after decades and decades of spinning their wheels.

The *Liberty* may not have defined my childhood the way it did for some of my siblings. It was always present, but it wasn't everything. What defined my childhood more was watching my Dad try, sometimes clumsily, sometimes imperfectly, to carry something heavy while still being a father.

I don't think he was perfect. I don't think he would claim to be. But I know he did the best he knew how to do with what he was carrying. And that matters.

People always ask if my Dad's story had anything to do with my path.

I became a Navy SEAL.

A Father's Reflection...

Listening to my children tell their stories was harder than anything I ever wrote to Congress.

I fought for the 34 men who never got to grow old. I marched. I wrote letters. I stood in front of the cameras. I told myself I was honoring them. And I was. But somewhere along the way, I didn't always see what my fight was costing the people still living under my roof.

The *Liberty* didn't just take 34 lives in 1967. It followed me home. It sat at our dinner table. It rode in the car with us. It showed up in my temper, in my drinking, in my silence.

Each of my children experienced a different version of me. Frankie saw instability. Dee saw intensity. Bryce felt pressure. Shane watched and adapted. And August felt distance.

I left Frankie and August for six years. There's no way to polish that. No explanation makes it easier for a little girl waiting for her father to come back. Trauma may explain behavior, but it does not erase impact. August and I are talking again now. Slowly. Carefully. Time does what it can. But relationships don't mend because you wish they would. They mend because you show up.

If this book does anything beyond honoring the 34, I hope it shows my children that I see them. I see what they carried. I see what I missed. I see the weight they bore while I was carrying my own. I used to believe my duty was only to the men who died beside me. Now I understand my duty was also to the ones who grew up beside me.

Staying afloat isn't just surviving what happens to you. It's making sure you didn't drown the people trying to swim with you. I understand that now.

Chapter 10: Pissing Into the Wind

When we walked out of the White House after being stood up by President George H. W. Bush, I knew something had shifted, just not in the way I had hoped. We believed that if we could get in front of the President of the United States and look him in the eye, something would move. We believed the truth, once spoken plainly, would demand action. Instead, we walked out with handshakes and nothing else. The machine just kept humming.

The 1990s and the 2000s didn't explode with dramatic confrontations or breaking news. They passed quietly on the surface, but underneath, I was still writing letters. Congressmen, Senators, Presidents, anyone who might be willing to reopen what had been buried. Most letters were never answered. The few that were answered felt like pre-written dismissals, polite and hollow.

It felt like pissing into the wind.

But even when letters aren't answered, I believe they were being read. I came to believe that with all my heart. Because sometimes you find out in ways you wish you hadn't. The silence wasn't indifference; it was containment. And containment is an active choice.

Dee mentioned this moment from her side. Here is what it looked like from mine. She was just a child, and children experience fear differently than adults do. It was one afternoon, when Dee was in first grade, that the phone rang. I picked it up, and a man's voice asked calmly, "Do you know where your daughter Deidre is?" He didn't say "Dee." He used her full name. Lisa was standing beside me, and the air in the room shifted instantly. Then he warned us to watch out for her.

Lisa immediately called the school and had Dee brought to the office. We picked her up ourselves. When someone says your child's name with that tone, it rewires you. You can tell yourself it's a prank or a bluff, but you don't take that chance. We never received confirmation of who it was, and they never needed to identify themselves. The message was clear enough.

The *Liberty* never left our house during those years. As my kids said, it sat at the kitchen table in the form of documents and notes. It lived in long phone calls and reunion planning. It followed me into my radio show, The *Liberty* Hour, where week after week I spoke into a microphone about what had happened and took calls from whoever was listening. When the mainstream didn't carry it, we built our own channel.

During that time, two Swedish industrialist brothers, Ted and Ben Grobe, read about the *Liberty* and decided to act. They were building a public library in Grafton, Wisconsin, and with our permission, they wanted to name it the **USS** *Liberty* Memorial Library. The decision triggered outrage and pressure from powerful corners. There were bomb threats and death threats ahead of the dedication ceremony. SWAT teams stood on rooftops when the building was opened to the public.

People tried to intimidate the town into changing the name. The letters on the building were initially made small, almost apologetic. The Grobe brothers demanded that they be made larger. The name stayed. That was the pattern of those years: quiet resistance met with quiet persistence.

The threats followed us in other ways. At reunions, strangers would corner men in elevators and mutter that we should shut up. Sometimes it felt random. Sometimes it felt planted. You learn to live with a constant low-grade alertness. It becomes background noise.

Years later, in 2009, when Shane was in BUD/S training to become a Navy SEAL, Lisa and I flew out to see him before graduation. We were sitting at a restaurant when a man approached me directly and identified me as "that **USS** *Liberty* guy." He wore a large watch and kept thrusting it toward my face. I didn't know if it was recording or something worse, and I pushed it away. The conversation escalated quickly. He told me the best thing I could do was keep my mouth shut. He claimed he was Mossad. Maybe he was telling the truth. Maybe he wanted me to believe he was. Either way, it was a threat.

Lisa had heard enough. She stood up, circled him, and confronted him in a way only a protective wife can. Her voice rose with every denial he offered, and eventually, security escorted us out instead of him. Later, we learned he had been at the hotel for days before we arrived. Who knows.

Other incidents are also hard to prove but harder to ignore. Once, while driving with Shane, the lug nuts on our truck had been loosened. The wheel began wobbling at highway speed, and we pulled over just in time before it came off. Maybe it was random vandalism. Maybe it wasn't. After years of threats, coincidence feels thinner.

Lisa carried her own burden. There were years when she was simply sick of the *Liberty*. Sick of reunions, sick of tension, sick of sharing her husband with an event that had ended before we met. She never threatened divorce, but there were times she hit a breaking point. Being married to a cause means your spouse shares the consequences.

Through all of it, I kept writing. Long before Bush, I had already written to President Reagan. As a Purple Heart and Bronze Star recipient, a U.S. Navy veteran, and a survivor of the **USS** *Liberty*, I asked for one simple thing: a real investigation and a congressional hearing.

This is what I received in return. March 20, 1986.

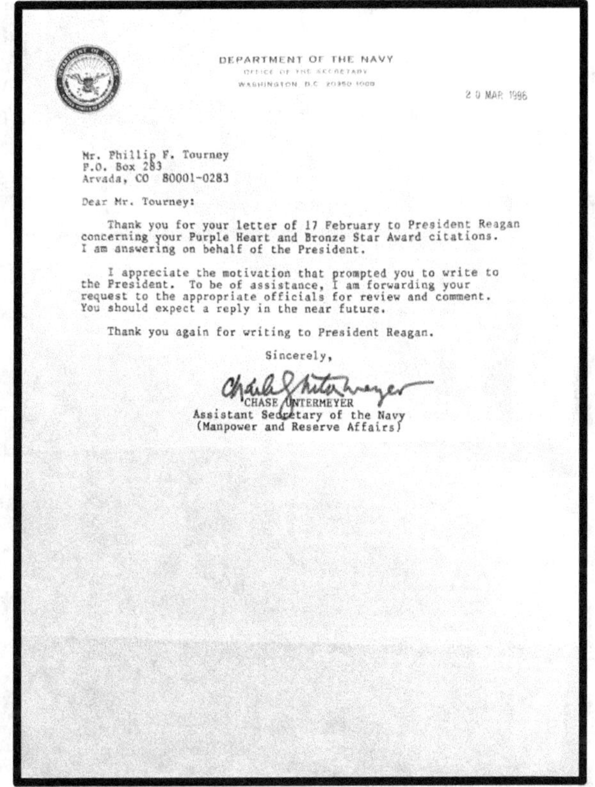

I am still waiting.

1986 was when I really began writing. This type of response became par for the course.

This particular one came from Congresswoman Patricia Schroeder of Denver's 1st District.

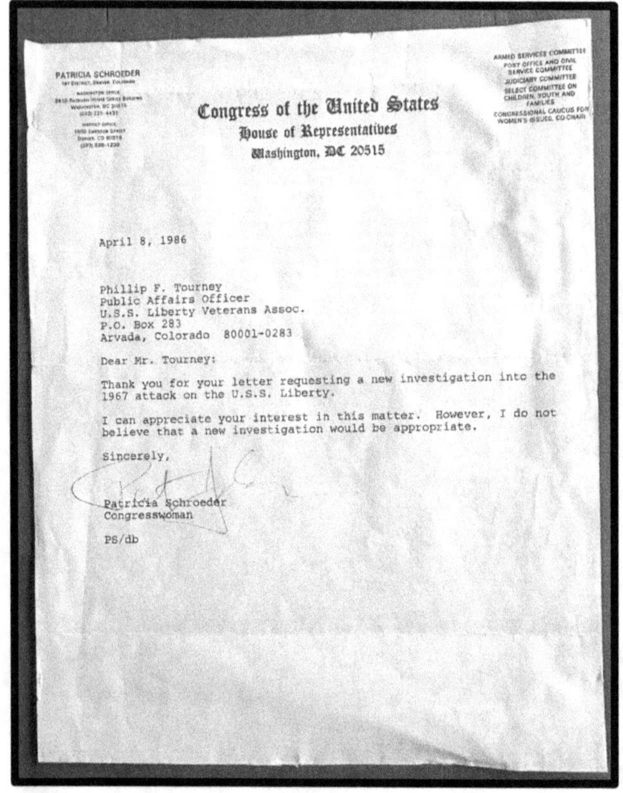

Polite. Dismissive. Final. But I never stopped. Presidents changed. Congress changed. Wars started and ended. Administrations came and went.

The letters did not. I kept going. These are not my recollections. They are my records. I kept copies of everything.

In 1994, I wrote to President Bill Clinton. By then, nearly three decades had passed since the attack. I was still asking for the same thing.

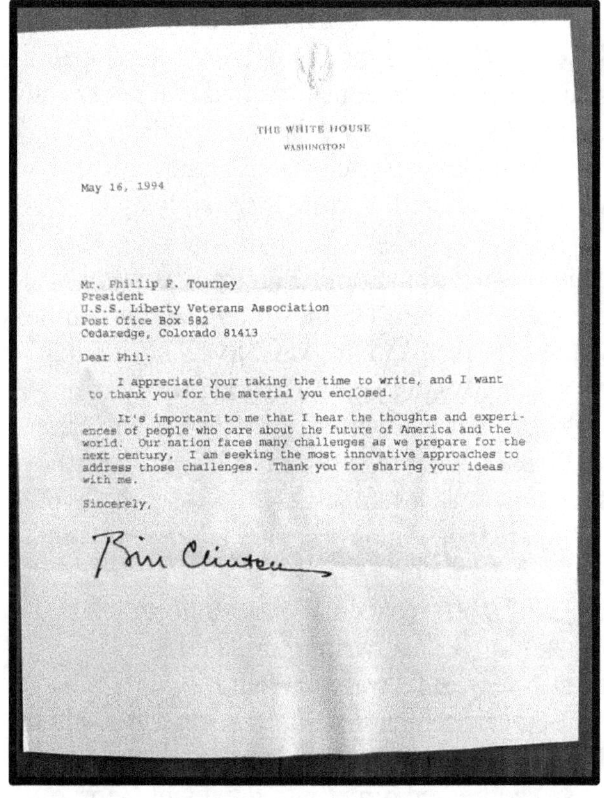

THE WHITE HOUSE
WASHINGTON

May 16, 1994

Mr. Phillip F. Tourney
President
U.S.S. Liberty Veterans Association
Post Ofice Box 582
Cedaredge, Colorado 81413

Dear Phil:

I appreciate your taking the time to write, and I want to thank you for the material you enclosed.

It's important to me that I hear the thoughts and experiences of people who care about the future of America and the world. Our nation faces many challenges as we prepare for the next century. I am seeking the most innovative approaches to address those challenges. Thank you for sharing your ideas with me.

Sincerely,

Bill Clinton

There were many more. Letters to presidents, senators, committee chairs, and anyone willing to read them. The full record spans decades. A selection of that correspondence appears in the appendix.

I did not write those letters casually. Each one took time, thought, and the willingness to relive June 8, 1967, all over again. Every envelope I sealed meant reopening a wound that never fully closed. I was not naïve about the odds. I understood how power works. I knew most would be ignored. I wrote them anyway.

This was not about politics for me. It was about the men who didn't come home and the families who never received answers. I was not asking for revenge, and I was not asking for sympathy. I was asking my government to look at the truth and have the courage to face it. If that meant spending decades knocking on a door that would not open, then that is what I was prepared to do.

By 2007, forty years had passed. Forty years. I was no longer just writing private letters. A friend stepped forward and paid to run a full-page advertisement in *The Washington Times* on June 8, 2007, the 40th anniversary of the attack. It was addressed directly to President George W. Bush. If my letters could be ignored quietly, this could not.

Advertisement   Advertisement   Advertisement

PRESIDENT BUSH – WE CAN'T HEAR YOU? YOUR SILENCE HAS BEEN DEAFENING!

Mr. President, five years and two years ago the survivors of the U.S.S. Liberty wrote the following letter. Once again we appeal to you. To date we have not heard one word from you!

In memory of those American sailors killed on the LIBERTY by Israel in international water on June 8, 1967

James Lee Lenau, Washington, Missouri

Raymond Eugene Linn, Adamsville, Ohio

James Mahlon Lupton, Shreveport, Louisiana

Duane Rowe Marggraf, Fond du Lac, Wisconsin

David Walter Marlborough, Waterville, Maine

Anthony Peter Mendle, Waterbury, Connecticut

Carl Christian Nygren, Williamsport, Pennsylvania

Jack Lewis Raper, Cedartown, Georgia

David NMN Skolak, Gary, Indiana

Edward Emory Rehmeyer, III, York, Pennsylvania

John Caleb Smith, Jr., Ithaca, New York

Melvin Douglas Smith, Alamance, North Carolina

John Clarence Spicher, Turnabum, Pennsylvania

Alexander Neil Thompson, Philadelphia, Pennsylvania

Thomas Roy Thornton, Springfield, Ohio

Philippe Charles Tiedtke, Santa Cruz, California

Frederick James Walton, Niagara Falls, New York

Philip McCutcheon Armstrong, Detroit, Michigan

James Cecil Pierce, Clinton, North Carolina

Stephen Spencer Toth, San Diego, California

Gary Ray Blanchard, Wichita, Kansas

William Bernard Allenbaugh, Baltimore, Maryland

Allen Merle Blue, Yakima, Washington

Francis [NMN] Brown, Albany, New York

Ronnie Jordon Campbell, Sevierville, Tennessee

Jerry Leroy Converse, Puyallup, Washington

Robert Burton Eisenberg, St. Paul, Minnesota

Jerry Lee Goss, North Vernon, Indiana

Lawrence Paul Hayden, Houston, Texas

Curtis Alan Graves, Grosse Pointe Farms, Michigan

Warren Edward Hersey, Philadelphia, Pennsylvania

Alan [NMN] Higgins, Weymouth, Massachusetts

Carl Lewis Hoar, Mount Vernon, Ohio

Richard Walter Keene, Jr., Batavia, New York

U.S.S. LIBERTY VETERANS ASSOCIATION
P. O. Box 1887, Washington DC 20013-1887

President George W. Bush , Commander In Chief
June 8, 2007 White House , Washington DC

Dear Mr. President,

Friday June 8, 2007 marks the 40th anniversary of probably the most shameful day in American history. That day America's banner and honor was treacherously trashed by our so-called ally, Israel. Thirty four Americans were brutally slaughtered, 172 wounded, including myself, and America's most sophisticated intelligence ship was so badly damaged it had to be scrapped. Israel deliberately attacked America's virtually unarmed USS LIBERTY in international waters, knowing full well our identity, in an assault that lasted as long as the attack on Pearl Harbor.

On that bright, sunny infamous day, the LIBERTY had a large American flag flapping in the wind and 10' high I.D. marking on her hull which were clearly visible during the full six hours (6:00 A.M. to 12:00 Noon) that low flying, slow moving, propeller recons distinctly marked with Star of Davids reconnoitered our ship. Overheard radio transmission of the pilots confirmed that the Israel had positively identified the LIBERTY as American.

Suddenly at 2:00 p.m., the government of Israel put a knife in the back of America. In a diabolic attempt at deception, the Israelis began the attack with unmarked jet fighters using rockets, canons, and napalm on our unprotected ship. Then three motor torpedo boats arrived on the scene and fired 5 torpedoes at us, one hitting its mark, midship's on the starboard side, instantly blowing to bits 25 of America's finest young men. The torpedo gunmen shot at our firefighters and stretcher bearers, using us as target practice, maiming and murdering as many of America's sons as they could.

The captain ordered us to prepare to abandon ship as the ship was in grave danger of sinking from torpedo hit that left a 40'x40' hole in her. There were only 3 life rafts left that they hadn't already destroyed. We put them over the side to put as many wounded in as possible. The torpedo boats machine gunned the life rafts and sank two of them and took one aboard their boat- no survivors were to be taken! Helicopters were overhead to board our ship with Israeli commandos at the ready to finish us off.

Responding to a S.O.S. from the LIBERTY, the USS SARATOGA launched their jets approximately 15 minutes into the vicious Israeli attack. Within minutes after the launch, incredibly and inexplicably, Washington shamefully and unconscionably recalled the jets, abandoning helpless American sailors under fire, and subjecting them to an additional two hours of barbaric Israeli bombardment and butchery.

Fortuitously when the Israelis picked up an invalid message that U.S. help was on the way, Israel reluctantly was forced to terminate its ongoing assault. Without that break, I would not be alive writing this letter.

Ironically help did not arrive until 18 hours after the attack when it was only 15 minutes away. When an American rescue ship finally arrived, what they found was shocking, the LIBERTY was in shambles, death on the water. There were 821 rocket and canon holes in her hull, thousands of 50 caliber armor piercing bullets riddling her skin, a funnel size torpedo cavity in her broad side, and the residue of napalm that had been dropped to burn us up. Blood and body parts were strewn across the deck. A sad , outrageous story, but unfortunately true.

The crew of the most decorated naval ship in American history was ordered to remain silent under threat of court martial, imprisonment or worse, and we all knew what worst meant. The U.S. government has never challenged the obviously phony Israeli excuse of "mistaken identity" nor have they attempted to expose the dishonorable cover up that continues to date. Truth and America's honor were ignominiously sacrificed to provide cover for Israel's transparent lies and despicable act of perfidy.

Israel's premeditated, sneak attack on the USS LIBERTY was a direct attack on America. The disgraceful refusal of unpatriotic American governmental officials of dubious allegiance to defend America and come to the aid of brave Americans under attack can only be characterized as treasonous.

Mr. President, on behalf of the courageous crew of the USS LIBERTY, dead and alive, I respectfully request that you commission a presidential panel to finally investigate the attack and cover-up of the USS LIBERTY, and report the truth to American people.

Thank you, Mr. President. God bless you! God bless America!

U.S.S. Liberty Press Conferences
Marriott Courtyard,
Tysons Corner, VA
June 8 & 9, 2007

Respectfully,

Philip F. Tourney, President
USS LIBERTY Veterans Association

"If American leaders did not have the courage to punish Israel for the lenient murder of American citizens, their American friends would let them get away with almost anything."
George Ball, Assistant Secretary of State , 1967

"The nation which indulges toward another ... it is some degree a slave ...
... a passionate attachment of one nation for another produces a variety of evils."
President George Washington Farewell Address September 17, 1796

Postscript

President George W. Bush
Commander In Chief

Dear Mr. President:

We have supported you as President and as Commander in Chief during difficult times for our nation. We expect that you would do the same for the brave survivors of the U.S.S. Liberty. Accordingly, we urge you to appoint the **first** ever open and independent panel to investigate the bloody attack on the Liberty. This is the third time that we have requested your help. The two previous times, we received pro-forma letters from a White House staffer alleging that the attack had already been investigated? This is a bald-faced lie! If your reply to our letter this time is the same or is non-responsive, we can only conclude that you are an acquiescent participant in the shameful cover up. We pray that this will not be the case. God bless you!

Sincerely,

Philip F. Tourney, President
USS LIBERTY Veterans Association

Analysis
Traitors, Cowards, and a "Parliament of Whores"*

What better words define and describe the disloyal and treasonous government officials, who on June 8, 1967 allowed over 200 American sailors on the unarmed U.S.S. Liberty to be murdered and wounded in broad daylight on international water in a deliberate attack by Israel aircraft and torpedo boats? Incredibly, these same subservient public officials, apparently owing their allegiance to a foreign entity, collaborated to protect a guilty Israel from public condemnation and punishment by manipulating and relegating the bloody massacre into a political black hole for four decades.

Traitors

President Lyndon B. Johnson and Secretary of Defense Robert Mc Namara qualified as co-perpetrators in treason by ordering and executing the pull back of American aircraft responding to desperate calls from the helpless Liberty crew, and permitting the massacre to continue. Finally, the co-conspirators initiated and orchestrated a criminal cover up that remains in place until today.

Cowards

Every one of the faceless, gutless government officials and bureaucrats who know the truth and dare not to act or speak out

"Parliament of Whores"*

*(Patrick J. Buchanan's incisive characterization of Congress's servile sellout relationship with Israel.)

To date Congress has fearfully evaded and defaulted on its oversight responsibility to conduct an independent and open investigation to expose the truth of the deliberate and unprovoked attack on the U.S.S. Liberty by Israel. In fact, no investigation has ever been held at any level of government to investigate the Israeli treachery. Israeli P.A.C.S. paid off Congress well for the pass-approximately $3,300,000.00 in the latest 2005-2006 election cycle, and over $50,000,000.00 since 1978. Of course a grateful Congress has reciprocated, haven given lavishly to the Mideast mini state over $100,000,000,000.00 of U.S. tax payers' money. A return on investment that would put Warren Buffet to shame. Enough!

We had gone public out of necessity. The full-page ad laid out, in plain terms, what happened on June 8, 1967: the USS *Liberty* was attacked in international waters, 34 Americans were killed. It stated that the survivors had repeatedly appealed to President Bush and received no reply, and it asked him to appoint a presidential panel to investigate both the attack and the long-running cover-up. The ad also memorialized the men who died.

Forty years of silence had become its own form of betrayal.

Even after going public like that, there was still no hearing, no investigation, and no public response from the White House. Forty years after the attack, the silence remained intact. It still does.

From 1990 to 2020, the **USS *Liberty*** still never broke into the mainstream in any meaningful way. No new investigation. No apology. No accountability. But my fight never stopped. It simply lived in the margins, where uncomfortable truths tend to wait.

For 30 years, I wrote, called, spoke, and showed up. The world moved on from 1967, but I never could. The ***Liberty*** didn't stay in the Mediterranean; it came home with me. And for three decades, I kept pushing against a wall that never seemed to crack.

My Reflection...

For a long time, I measured success by noise. I thought if I could just get loud enough, write enough letters, make enough calls, someone in power would finally have to respond. What I didn't understand was that silence can be a strategy. The absence of acknowledgment doesn't mean you're not being heard. Sometimes it means you're being ignored, on purpose.

Those 30 years after the White House non-meeting were some of the hardest in a different way than 1967. On the ship, you know who the enemy is. At home, it's fog. It's unanswered mail. It's a polite dismissal. It's threats that can't be proven and fear that can't be publicly validated. You begin to question whether you're crazy for continuing.

But every threat, every strange encounter, every warning to "shut up" told me something important. It told me the story still mattered. It told me somebody, somewhere, didn't want it told. If the *Liberty* had truly been meaningless, no one would have bothered to intimidate a nameless former sailor writing letters from his kitchen table.

The cost, though, was not imaginary. My children grew up with tension in the air. Lisa grew tired of competing with ghosts of 1967. I was fighting a government, but sometimes it spilled into my home in ways I didn't fully see at the time. Trauma doesn't stay contained to the original battlefield.

There were moments I wondered if I should just stop. Just be a husband. Just be a father. Just let history do what it does and fade. But every time I thought about quitting, I pictured the 34 men who never got that option. I remembered that they didn't get to grow old. They didn't get to raise children. They didn't get to argue with their wives about reunions.

So, I kept writing. I kept calling. I kept showing up to events where most people had never heard of the **USS *Liberty***. I wasn't chasing fame or recognition. I was chasing accountability, even if it never came in my lifetime.

Looking back, I realize something else. Persistence is not glamorous. It is repetitive. It is lonely. It is often humiliating. But it is also the only reason truth survives long enough for the next generation to find it.

For 30 years, it felt like nothing was happening. In reality, everything was building. Every letter,

every radio show, every confrontation, every
threat, it all stacked quietly. Sometimes history
doesn't break open with one moment.
Sometimes it erodes slowly until the wall finally
gives way.

What I didn't know was that the wall was closer
to giving way than I thought.

And that the crack would come from the most
unexpected place: a letter to a woman I had
never met.

Chapter 11: The Letter

I was seventy-seven years old when I wrote the letter to Candace Owens. I had written to presidents, senators, and committee chairs for decades, but this felt different. I wasn't writing to power. I was writing to a person. I told myself it was just another letter, but deep down I knew I was taking one more shot before time ran out.

I began simply: "My name is Phillip Tourney. I am 77 years old." I told her I was a **USS *Liberty*** survivor and the President of the **USS *Liberty*** Veterans Association. In the letter, I described the morning of June 8, 1967. The sea was calm. The sky was clear. We were in international waters, more than twelve miles off the Sinai coast.

The American flag was flying high. I wrote that it was "a 5 by 8 flag very visible." There was nothing covert about our presence. We were a United States Navy ship conducting intelligence operations, plainly marked and openly sailing. I explained how our ship was not disguised, and it could not have been a case of mistaken identity.

That morning, reconnaissance aircraft circled us repeatedly. They were close enough for us to see the pilots inside the cockpits. "We would wave at them," I later told Candace. "They'd wave at us." There was no confusion about who we were.

At approximately 2:00 p.m., that changed.

The first jets came in low and fast. There was no warning. No radio contact. No attempt to identify us. "They hit every watertight door," I said in the interview. Rockets tore through the hull. Cannon fire ripped across the decks. Then came the napalm.

Napalm does not burn like wood or paper. It clings. It rolls across steel and skin alike. I told her, "You can't imagine. Every second was like an hour." The attack from the air lasted roughly twenty-five minutes. They targeted our communications first. Every antenna was shot away. They wanted us isolated.

One radioman, Terry Halbardier, crawled across the deck under fire to rig a temporary antenna. The distress signal went out: "Rockstar, Rockstar under attack by an unknown jet aircraft. Help us." Somehow, against the odds, it got through.

Rescue aircraft launched from the USS Saratoga.

Then they were recalled.

"Before the jets hit the horizon, they were recalled by Secretary of Defense Robert McNamara," I said. They were launched again. Recalled again. I told Candace what we had been later told, a quote attributed to President Lyndon Johnson: "I don't give a damn if all those sailors die. I'm not going to embarrass my ally, Israel."

She leaned forward when I said that. "So, he knew," she said.

"Yes," I answered. "He knew."

After the jets left, three torpedo boats approached. I remember feeling relief. I thought help had finally arrived.

Instead, they opened fire.

They circled us at close range, spraying the decks. Then came the torpedo. Over the loudspeaker, I heard, "Prepare for torpedo hit, starboard side."

The explosion tore through the communications spaces. Twenty-five men were killed instantly. In total, 34 Americans died that day, and at least 171 would be wounded, including myself.

The ship listed hard to starboard. For a moment, I believed we were going to roll over and sink.

"It felt like the hand of God was holding us up," I said. Life rafts were lowered into the water in case we had to abandon ship. The torpedo boats fired on them. That is something we watched happen. We were left in the Mediterranean for seventeen hours.

Candace asked what that felt like. I told her, "It felt like being lost." Two-thirds of the crew were dead or wounded. We were bleeding, burned, and in shock. I remember holding a sailor named Gary Blanchard. He looked at me and asked, "You think I'm going to die?"

"Yeah," I said. "I think you are."

He died in my arms.

Days later, Admiral Isaac Kidd boarded the ship. I remember him taking his stars off and saying, "I'm just like your dad. Please tell me everything you saw." We told him about the jets, the napalm, the torpedo boats, and the life rafts.

Then he put his stars back on. "You better never talk about this again to anybody, or I'll make sure you end up in prison, or worse."

I obeyed that order for nearly twenty years. "I didn't even tell my wife I was ever in the military," I told Candace. The silence became part of me.

Halfway through the interview, she said something that mattered. "I had never learned about the **USS *Liberty*** and its entire context until I received your letter." Then she added, "I'm genuinely embarrassed at my ignorance." That was when I realized something important, not that the battle was won, and not that history had suddenly changed, but that someone was actually listening.

Then she did something I never expected. "I want to pledge to you that personally, my family will donate $40,000 every year to your organization." The interview lasted nearly three hours, and it wasn't political theater. It was testimony.

I told her what happened. I told her what we were told. I told her what we lived with. When the cameras shut off, I went home not knowing if any of it would matter. Regardless, she was so kind to me.

My Reflection…

As I shared, by the time I wrote that letter, I was seventy-seven years old. For most of my life, I believed that if you wanted truth recognized, you had to go through official channels. You wrote letters, requested hearings, and appealed to authority. You waited for institutions to decide whether your story deserved attention.

But the world had changed. The gatekeepers were no longer the only way in, and the flow of information no longer depended on sealed envelopes or committee approvals. Somewhere along the way, the conversation had moved elsewhere.

I realized that if I truly wanted the story of the **USS *Liberty*** to be heard, I had to meet people where they were listening. That meant stepping into a world I didn't fully understand: podcasts, online platforms, and independent media. It was unfamiliar territory for a man who once trusted letters more than microphones.

Candace did something very few people in power have done. She listened, not just politely, or strategically, but with curiosity and humility. She did not owe me that interview, and she did not owe us her platform. Yet she opened it anyway and treated the 34 men we lost with respect.

At seventy-seven, I understood something I probably should have learned earlier. The truth does not disappear, but it does require persistence. When the method changes, you either adapt or you fade with the old system.

I chose to adapt.

Chapter 12: When the Wall Finally Gave

For thirty years, I had pushed against the silence that never seemed to move. Letters, interviews, radio shows, reunions. It often felt like knocking on a door that no one intended to open. I never knew when the spark would come. I just knew I had to keep knocking.

The spark came in the form of a letter. And the story about June 8, 1967, the one that had lived inside me for nearly six decades, was finally about to reach beyond my small circle.

The interview was not live. It aired days later, and when it did, things moved quickly. Within hours, clips were everywhere. My phone started ringing. Text messages came in. Emails. Donations began coming into the L.V.A. website, so many that the system couldn't handle it, and the site went offline.

Messages were coming in from across the country, and then from outside the country. Over the next twenty-four hours, it didn't slow down. People were listening. And they were responding. For the first time, millions of Americans were hearing a survivor recount the morning of June 8, 1967, without it being filtered through a government summary. For the first time, someone with a national platform like Candace Owens said publicly, "This has completely changed a lot for me." That mattered more than I expected.

But what struck me most was not how quickly it spread. It was how many Americans had no idea the **USS *Liberty*** had ever been attacked. The messages weren't political. They weren't angry. They weren't arguing about details. They were simple. "I've never heard of this." "How did I not know about this?" "Why weren't we ever taught this?"

That's when I understood what I'd really been up against.

It wasn't just disagreement over what happened. It wasn't just people accepting an official explanation. Most Americans had never even been introduced to the story. They didn't reject it. They had never been given the chance to.

Think about that.

34 Americans killed. At least 171 wounded. A United States Navy ship attacked for nearly two hours in international waters. And generations of Americans went through school without ever hearing the name **USS *Liberty***.

That doesn't happen by accident.

For years, we were told the public knew and had moved on. That wasn't true. The public didn't move on. The public was never brought in.

If something isn't in the textbooks, if it isn't discussed in classrooms, if it isn't covered honestly in mainstream media, then most people will never stumble across it on their own. That's just reality. And that's what I had been fighting all those years.

Not just an official explanation. A system that made sure most Americans would never even know there was a story to question.

When young veterans wrote to me and said, "Sir, we were never taught this," that hit me the hardest. These were men and women who wore the same uniform I did. And no one had thought it important enough to tell them about a Navy ship that nearly went to the bottom of the Mediterranean.

That's when I started asking a harder question. How does something like that disappear?

How does an attack on an American ship become a footnote so small that most citizens never see it? How does it get left out of the broader conversation about military history, about foreign policy, about accountability?

I don't pretend to know every answer. But I do know this: if people don't know something happened, they can't ask questions about it. They can't demand accountability. They can't even form an opinion. You can't argue about what you've never been told.

And for more than fifty years, most Americans were never told. At least now, they couldn't say they didn't know.

And that mattered.

For a long time, I believed the fight was about proving our side of the story. I thought if I could just get the right committee, the right hearing, the right investigation, then the truth would finally be acknowledged. I spent three decades knocking on those doors.

But now, I realized something had changed. I no longer needed permission to speak.

Social media and independent platforms had opened a door that never existed before. You didn't have to wait for a network to invite you. You didn't have to wait for a congressional hearing to be scheduled. You could simply tell the story.

That changed everything for me.

I wasn't trying to convince Washington anymore. I wasn't trying to force an institution to admit anything. I just wanted Americans to hear what happened and make up their own minds.

Let them read it. Let them listen. Let them decide.

If they believe it was a case of mistaken identity, that's their decision. If they believe it was something more, that's their decision too. My job was no longer to win an argument. My job was to tell the truth as I lived it.

For years, the system had controlled who got heard and who didn't. Now that control wasn't as tight as it used to be. And at seventy-seven years old, I decided I wasn't going to waste whatever time I had left arguing over access.

I was going to speak. Not louder. Just more directly.

And I was going to trust the American people to think for themselves.

My Reflection...

For most of my life, I believed that truth depended on authority. I believed that if something was true, the right institution would eventually recognize it. That if you kept presenting the facts long enough, someone in power would stand up and correct the record.

I was wrong about that.

Institutions do not always correct themselves. Systems do not always reward honesty. Sometimes truth survives not because it is acknowledged, but because ordinary people refuse to let it disappear.

That took me a long time to understand.

When I was young, I thought loyalty meant protecting the system. As I got older, I realized loyalty sometimes means challenging it. Not because you hate your country, but because you love it enough to want it to be better.

The **USS *Liberty*** was never just about what happened on June 8, 1967. It became a test of whether Americans were allowed to know uncomfortable things about their own history. And for decades, most of them were never even given the chance.

For thirty years, I carried anger.

Not loud anger. Not the kind that shouts. But the kind that sits in your chest for years. The kind that comes from feeling dismissed. From watching 34 men fade into footnotes while the official story stayed neat and convenient.

I told myself the anger was necessary. That it kept me going. That it fueled the fight. But somewhere along the way, I realized something: the anger wasn't helping me anymore.

It wasn't changing the system. It wasn't bringing justice. It wasn't honoring the 34 men we lost the way I thought it was. All it was doing was keeping me locked in the same battle.

When the interview aired, and Americans began saying, "We never knew," something shifted inside me. I stopped trying to force the country to admit something. I started wanting the country to simply hear it.

That's a different battle altogether. Anger tries to win. Clarity just tells the truth. Once I let go of the need to prove anything, I felt lighter. I didn't need Washington to agree with me. I didn't need a formal apology to validate what I had lived through. I needed Americans to know it happened.

And then I needed to trust them.

Trust them to think. Trust them to question.
Trust them to decide.

At seventy-seven years old, I stopped speaking
for recognition. I started speaking for
remembrance. That was the clarity. I cannot
control what institutions do. I cannot rewrite
history books. I cannot go back to June 8, 1967.

But I can tell the story. Calmly. Directly.
Without bitterness. And I can let people do what
free people are supposed to do. Think for
themselves.

That is up to the American people.

Chapter 13: Think for Yourself

When I was a young sailor, information moved in one direction. The government spoke. The networks reported. The newspapers printed. Most of us assumed that if something mattered, we would hear about it.

That was the system we trusted. If it made the evening news, it was important. If it didn't, we assumed it probably wasn't. Very few people questioned how stories were chosen or why some never surfaced.

When we pulled into Malta after the attack, we were wounded, exhausted, and still trying to understand what had just happened. The ship was torn apart. 34 men were dead. Others were barely holding on. But even then, the message from above was clear: keep quiet.

It was the same thing when I returned to the United States. There was no national debate. No investigative panels on television. No journalists demanding answers on camera. The official explanation was given, and most Americans accepted it without ever hearing from the men who had actually been there.

That was how the country operated at the time.

People trusted institutions. They trusted the chain of command. They trusted the press. In many cases, that trust had been earned over generations. Questioning authority was not common, and it was not encouraged.

Looking back now, I understand why most Americans never heard about the **USS *Liberty***. They weren't hiding from it. They weren't avoiding it. They simply trusted that if something that serious had happened, they would have been told.

But history shows us that blind spots exist.

Remember Operation Northwoods. It was a real proposal in the early 1960s suggesting staged incidents to justify military action. It was never carried out, but it was documented. The fact that it was even proposed reminds us that governments, like all institutions, are run by human beings capable of flawed judgment and having their own interests in mind.

Remember the Gulf of Tonkin. What was presented to the American public as a clear act of aggression later turned out to be far more complicated than originally described. That incident helped justify a war that cost tens of thousands of American lives.

These are not conspiracy theories. They are part of the historical record.

They remind us that institutions can make decisions behind closed doors, and that official explanations are not always the full story in the moment.

More recently, the attacks on September 11th became one of the most scrutinized events in modern history. Some people questioned aspects of the official narrative from the beginning. Others accepted it without hesitation. Over time, especially with the growth of social media, more Americans began examining technical reports, timelines, and unanswered questions.

Whether one agrees with those questions or not is not the point. The point is that the culture changed.

In the 1960s, questioning official accounts was rare and often discouraged. But that culture of deference did not end there. It carried through the 1970s, the 1980s, the 1990s, and even into the early 2000s. Most Americans still relied on a handful of networks and major newspapers to tell them what mattered.

If those outlets did not pursue a story, it rarely gained traction. The gatekeepers still controlled the flow. For decades, that structure shaped what the public knew and what it didn't.

Then technology changed everything.

The internet loosened the grip. Social media shattered it. Independent platforms gave ordinary people the ability to publish, question, and investigate in ways that simply did not exist when I came home from Malta.

That is the real paradigm shift.

In the old system, the risk was not knowing enough. In this system, the risk is believing too quickly. Noise spreads faster than truth. Outrage travels faster than evidence.

Thinking for yourself does not mean rejecting everything. It does not mean assuming every institution lies. And it does not mean believing the loudest voice in the room.

It means asking questions carefully. It means examining evidence patiently. It means being willing to look at facts that may challenge your assumptions without immediately turning them into ammunition.

When I came home from Malta, very few people questioned what they were told. That was the culture. Today, almost everything is questioned. That can feel chaotic, but it can also be healthy, if it is done with discipline. Free people are not just free to speak. They are free to think. And thinking requires effort. It requires humility. It requires a willingness to sit with complexity instead of rushing to simple answers.

If Americans had been given the full story about the **USS *Liberty*** from the beginning, they could have examined it. They could have debated it. They could have drawn their own conclusions.

But you cannot think critically about something you have never been allowed to see. That is the lesson I learned late in life.

The truth does not belong to institutions. It does not belong to politicians. It does not belong to television networks or online platforms.

It belongs to the people. But only if they are willing to seek it out. Democracy does not survive on blind trust. It also does not survive on permanent outrage. It survives when citizens are informed, thoughtful, and willing to examine facts carefully.

When I say, "That is up to the American people," I mean it. Not as a slogan. But as a responsibility.

My Reflection…

For most of my life, I lived inside the old system. I trusted it because that is what my generation was taught to do. We believed institutions, even flawed ones, ultimately corrected themselves.

Coming home from Malta, I did not question why the story of what happened to us faded so quickly. I assumed someone above my pay grade had decided how it needed to be handled. That was the culture, and I accepted it. It took me decades to realize that silence is not always accidental. Sometimes it is structural. Sometimes it is simply easier not to revisit uncomfortable things.

I do not regret my loyalty to this country. I never have. But I have learned that loyalty and indifference are not the same thing.

Thinking for yourself does not mean tearing everything down. It means caring enough to examine what you are being told. It means loving your country enough to want it to be honest with itself. It also means being honest with yourself and putting yourself in other people's shoes.

If I could go back to the young sailor stepping off the **USS *Liberty*** from Malta, I would tell him something simple: do not be afraid to ask questions. I tell you the same thing now.

Not angrily. Not recklessly. But courageously. Because free people are not defined by what they are told.

They are defined by what they are willing to examine.

Chapter 14: The Whirlwind

The days after the interview aired were unlike anything I had experienced in nearly six decades. The phone did not stop ringing. Emails came in faster than I could answer them. Donations hit levels the USS Liberty Veterans Association had never seen before.

But what surprised me most was not the money. It was the invitations.

Podcast after podcast reached out asking me to come on and tell the story. Fight Back with Jake Shields. Deep Shallow Dive. Redacted with Clayton Morris. Breaking Points with guest host James Li. The Jimmy Dore Show. The Scott Ritter Show. The Scott Horton Show. The BermPit Podcast. JSlay USA with Jeremy Slayden. Revolutionary Change Podcast. And many others.

They were not asking me to prove anything or convince anybody. They just wanted me to tell my story to their audience. For years, we had struggled just to get a hearing. Now I was trying to keep up with the requests, and it felt like something had cracked open.

I owed all of that to Candace. We all did.

Going on Candace Owens was the modern equivalent of appearing on a program like 60 Minutes. The reach was national. The audience was engaged. But what happened afterward was something entirely new.

Instead of a single broadcast that aired once and faded, the interview multiplied. Thousands of people clipped segments of the conversation. They took pieces of what I said, pieces of what she said, and built their own short videos around them.

They added commentary. They added context. They added their own perspective. Each clip became a new starting point. And every time one of those clips circulated, the conversation began again.

This was not the old media cycle. It did not move in one straight line. It branched, repeated, and expanded. That was the new playing field. The gatekeepers were no longer deciding how long the story lived. The audience was.

At the same time, the world itself was shifting.

The war in Gaza dominated screens across America, both large and small. But what made this moment different was not just the coverage.

It was the unfiltered images streaming directly onto people's phones in real time.

For many Americans, especially Gen Z and younger Millennials, this was the first time they had watched a conflict unfold without relying on a nightly broadcast to interpret it for them. For Gen X and Baby Boomers, it was the first time a war was experienced without waiting for the evening news to frame the narrative.

No gatekeepers were deciding which thirty seconds would air at 6:30 p.m. The footage circulated instantly, and people formed impressions before traditional institutions had time to respond.

That changed the rhythm of public conversation. That shift did not stay confined to Gaza. It spilled into broader questions about history, alliances, and accountability. People began questioning long-held assumptions. They began asking harder questions about our foreign policy, those alliances, and the role of the United States overseas. Conversations that once stayed at the margins moved into the mainstream.

I could see that a broader conversation was taking place. Americans were reconsidering what they had been told for decades about who our allies were, what our interests were, and how decisions were made. The younger generations, especially Gen Z, did not automatically inherit the old assumptions. They were willing to question them openly. That willingness changed the tone of the national conversation.

And in that environment, the **USS *Liberty*** resurfaced. Or maybe I should say, surfaced.

People began asking one simple question. If Israel is described as America's greatest ally, why did it attack an American ship in 1967? Why had they never heard about it? Why had it never been fully debated in public? Those questions were not framed as blame. They reflected a simple desire to know what had really happened.

The country was also already in the middle of a larger shift. In 2024, many voters believed they were choosing a more "America First" approach to foreign policy. They expected less involvement overseas and more focus at home. In 2025, when reality did not always align neatly with those expectations, more questions followed.

And in the middle of that questioning, the **USS *Liberty*** story was relevant. Not because it was new, but because it had never been fully examined or even discussed. For decades, the

Liberty had been treated as something settled. Something minor. Something already explained.

In many ways, it had not even been treated at all. It wasn't debated. It wasn't revisited. It wasn't meaningfully examined in classrooms or widely discussed in public forums. For many Americans, it simply did not exist in their understanding of history. Now it was.

What I witnessed was not outrage. It was curiosity. People were not coming to me with conclusions. They were coming with questions. That is very different. Social media did not create the questions. It made them visible.

And for the first time in fifty-eight years, the story of the **USS *Liberty*** was being discussed alongside modern debates about accountability, transparency, and foreign policy. It was a convergence. A long-buried event. A changing media landscape. A country rethinking its assumptions. And a generation willing to examine uncomfortable parts of history.

I did not create that moment. I simply stepped into it. And for the first time, I felt like the country was ready to listen.

My Reflection…

For most of my life, I carried the **Liberty** story like a burden. It felt heavy. It felt unfinished. It felt like something that had never been given daylight. When the interview aired and everything that followed began to unfold, I did not feel what I expected to feel. I did not feel victory. I felt something closer to relief.

For decades, I had believed that recognition had to come from the top. From institutions. From official statements. From the same system that had once gone quiet. But what I witnessed in those months after Candace showed me that the old system no longer had the final word.

Truth does not always rise because it is approved. Sometimes it rises because people are ready to hear it.

I also realized something else, even more important. The story no longer belonged only to us, the men who lived it. The survivors. It belonged to the country now. Once millions of Americans heard it, once thousands began sharing it and discussing it, it stopped being something confined to reunions and veterans' gatherings. It became part of a national conversation. That changed me.

And for the first time in nearly sixty years, I felt like the 34 men we lost were not alone in memory anymore. They were being remembered by people who had never even heard their names before.

That meant more to me than any official apology ever could. For decades, I had been pushing against a wall. Now I understood that sometimes you don't push through a wall. You wait until the ground shifts underneath it.

The ground had shifted.

Chapter 15: The Young Man in the Photo

Sometimes I look at that photograph taken in 1966 aboard the **USS _Liberty_**. I was twenty years old, wearing a clean uniform and doing my job, the way young men and women have done it in every generation. I looked like every kid who joins the military believing in something, believing the rules will be followed, and believing their country will tell them the truth. I didn't know how fast life can split into before and after.

I had no idea what was coming.

I did not know that in less than a year I would watch the sky fill with fire. I did not know I would lose friends in a matter of minutes. I did not know that surviving the attack would be only the beginning, and that the silence afterward would last longer than the smoke.

If I could stand next to that young sailor now, I would not warn him. I would not tell him to run. I would not try to rewrite his path. I would simply tell him the truth, the kind of truth you only learn by living it: you are going to survive.

And that survival is not the end of the story.

You are going to carry 34 names for the rest of your life. You are going to carry questions that do not have clean answers. You are going to carry anger for a long time, and for a while, it will feel like fuel. You are going to believe that if you push hard enough, the right people will eventually do the right thing.

But one day you will learn to set that anger down. You will learn that telling the truth calmly is stronger than shouting it. You will learn that the point is not to win an argument, but to refuse to give up on what you know. You will learn that time moves slowly, but it does move.

For years, I thought staying afloat meant pushing constantly. Writing. Calling. Arguing. Trying to force a door open that was never meant to open. I believed that if I just worked hard enough, someone with authority would finally correct the record.

Now I understand something different.

Sometimes staying afloat means holding steady long enough for the current to change. It means not giving up when nothing seems to move. It means keeping your balance while the world catches up.

That photograph is not just a picture of a young sailor. It is a reminder of what remains when the noise dies down. Names. Faces. A ship that should have sunk, but didn't. A story that should have disappeared, but didn't.

I cannot change what happened on June 8, 1967. I cannot give the 34 men back the lives they should have lived. But I can refuse to let them be erased.

I could not stop the attack. I could not stop the silence. But I could refuse to let this story sink.

That is what I did.

One Last Thing…

If you finished this book, you now know something most Americans were never taught. You know what happened to the **USS *Liberty*** and what happened afterward, the silence, the threats, the decades of dismissal, and the long fight just to be heard.

But this book is not only about a ship.

It is about what happens when truth becomes inconvenient, and how easily a story can disappear when institutions decide it should. It is also about what it costs the people who carry that story, not just the survivors, but their families as well.

I did not write this to make anyone angry. I wrote it so the 34 men we lost would not be erased, and so the American people could decide for themselves what they believe.

My Reflection…

I wish none of this had ever happened. I wish I had never had a reason to write this book. I wish June 8, 1967, had been just an ordinary day.

But if this story meant something to you, do one simple thing. Tell someone about it.

Thank you for spending this time with me.

Phil

The End.

… but also, the beginning.

Epilogue

By Lisa Tourney

When you live with a man who survived something like the **USS *Liberty***, you don't just marry the man. You marry what happened to him.

I didn't know that when I met Phil. I knew he was hardworking and stubborn, and I knew he had a quiet side that could make you feel like part of him was somewhere else, even while he sat right in front of you. What I didn't know was that there was a ship living inside him, and that it carried 34 names.

For a long time, I didn't even know he had been in the Navy. Phil wasn't hiding something from me. He was still living under the orders and threats that had been placed on him by his superiors after the attack. Keep your mouth shut or else. He was just doing what he had been taught to do for years after the attack: keep quiet and keep moving. That kind of silence doesn't end just because life goes on. It follows you home.

When I finally learned what happened, I understood two things immediately. First, that

June 8, 1967, would never be "over" for him. Second, that if he ever started telling the story, it would become part of our lives in a way most people would never understand.

I was right.

There were years when I felt like I was sharing my husband with a ship. Not in a symbolic way. In a real way. The phone calls. The letters. The meetings. The reunions. The **Liberty** followed us into our home and into our marriage.

Sometimes it wore him down. Sometimes it hardened him. Sometimes it made him angry. And if I'm being honest, there were times it made me angry as well. I didn't sign up for the politics, the threats, or the endless frustration of watching doors stay closed for decades.

But I did sign up for Phil. And you cannot separate Phil from what he lived through.

People who don't understand that sometimes describe him as obsessive, as if he just couldn't let something go. They don't see what he carries. They don't see what it does to a man to live through something violent and then be told it didn't happen the way he knows it happened. They don't see what it does to him to watch the world move on while the men he lost are treated like an afterthought.

Phil didn't keep going because he wanted attention. He kept going because he could not live with letting it disappear.

I watched him try to build a normal life. I watched him work, provide, laugh, and be a father. I also watched the **Liberty** return in waves, sometimes quietly and sometimes like a storm. Survivor's guilt is not something you "get over." It changes shape, but it doesn't vanish.

What I want you to know after reading this book is that Phil is not writing to recruit you to his side. He is not writing to argue politics. He is writing because truth matters, and because the 34 men who died deserve to be remembered with honesty.

If you felt anger while reading, I understand. If you felt sadness, I understand. If you felt disbelief, I understand. I have felt all of it at different times.

But above all, I hope you felt respect. Respect for the men who didn't come home. Respect for the survivors who carried the story for decades. And respect for the difficult, stubborn work of refusing to let the truth sink just because it is inconvenient.

This book is Phil's memory on paper. It is the story he lived, told as plainly as he can tell it. And if you are holding this book, it means you are now part of what he fought for all these years. Thank you for reading his story.

Lisa Tourney

About the Author

Phillip F. Tourney is a decorated United States Navy veteran and one of the last surviving crew members of the USS *Liberty*. Before the *Liberty*, he completed two tours of duty aboard the USS *Mauna Kea* in waters off Vietnam. For his heroic actions aboard the USS *Liberty* on June 8, 1967, Phil was awarded the **Bronze Star with "V" Device for Valor** and the **Purple Heart**. 34 of his shipmates were killed that day. Phil survived.

That day could have defined him by tragedy. Instead, it became the foundation of his purpose. Phil has served as a multiple-term President of the **USS Liberty Veterans Association**, spending more than five decades demanding a full and independent congressional investigation into the attack. He has never stopped asking the questions the government has never fully answered.

Today, Phil carries two missions: to honor the memory of the 34 men who gave their lives aboard the **USS *Liberty***, and to inspire others to live with courage, faith, and perseverance. Through his podcast, his speaking, and now this book, Phil has turned a lifetime of pain into a message that reaches anyone who has ever faced a storm they weren't sure they could survive. He is the host of *The Phil Tourney Podcast* and a sought-after motivational speaker, bringing his story to veterans, students, and audiences across the country.

He is available for speaking engagements at **www.philtourneypodcast.com**.

"They tried to sink us. We stayed afloat.

And that's what life demands…

STAY AFLOAT."

— **Phil Tourney**

USS Liberty Survivor • US Navy Veteran • Patriot

**Honoring the Past.
Inspiring the Future.**

Appendix

Letter issued for the President by Admiral John S. McCain Jr., Commander in Chief of United States Naval Forces Europe in 1967

The President of the United States takes pleasure in presenting the BRONZE STAR MEDAL to

PETTY OFFICER THIRD CLASS PHILLIP FRANCIS TOURNEY
UNITED STATES NAVY

for service as set forth in the following

CITATION:

"For heroic achievement in connection with the unprovoked and unexpected armed attack on USS Liberty (AGTR 5) in the Eastern Mediterranean on 8 June 1967. During the early afternoon hours, USS Liberty, while engaged in peaceful operations in international waters, was attacked without warning by jet fighter aircraft and three motor torpedo boats. The Liberty was subjected to intense incendiary, machine gun, and rocket fire and was placed in extreme jeopardy by a torpedo hit below the waterline on the starboard side in the vicinity of the Research compartment. Severe structural damage and extensive personnel casualties were incurred. Petty Officer Tourney, serving as Assistant on Scene Leader in the Forward Repair Party, first assisted in organizing the evacuation of wounded personnel from the exposed weather decks. With complete disregard for his own personal safety he continued to fearlessly expose himself to intense rocket and machine gun fire to move a fire fighting team to the bridge. He then returned to the forward weather decks to insure that no more wounded were still exposed before going below to maintain damage control conditions of compartments below the waterline. He remained below decks during the torpedo attack and immediately afterward assisted and directed emergency repairs to minimize further flooding and damage. His aggressiveness and coolness under fire was exceptional inspirational leadership in an hour of awesome peril. Petty Officer Tourney's initiative and courageous actions were in keeping with the highest traditions of the United States Naval Service."

Petty Officer Tourney is authorized to wear the Combat "V".

For the President

JOHN S. McCAIN, JR.
Admiral, United States Navy
Commander in Chief, United States Naval Forces, Europe

Letter from the American-Arab Anti-Discrimination Committee (ADC), October 7, 1985

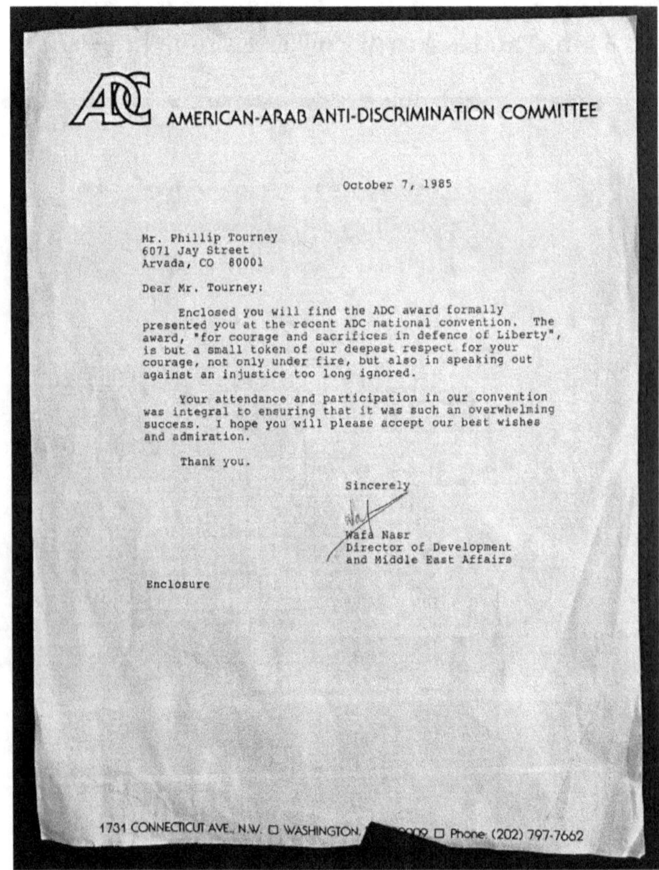

AMERICAN-ARAB ANTI-DISCRIMINATION COMMITTEE

October 7, 1985

Mr. Phillip Tourney
6071 Jay Street
Arvada, CO 80001

Dear Mr. Tourney:

Enclosed you will find the ADC award formally presented you at the recent ADC national convention. The award, "for courage and sacrifices in defence of Liberty", is but a small token of our deepest respect for your courage, not only under fire, but also in speaking out against an injustice too long ignored.

Your attendance and participation in our convention was integral to ensuring that it was such an overwhelming success. I hope you will please accept our best wishes and admiration.

Thank you.

Sincerely

Wafa Nasr
Director of Development
and Middle East Affairs

Enclosure

1731 CONNECTICUT AVE., N.W. □ WASHINGTON, □ 9009 □ Phone: (202) 797-7662

Letter from Congresswoman Patricia Schroeder, April 8, 1986

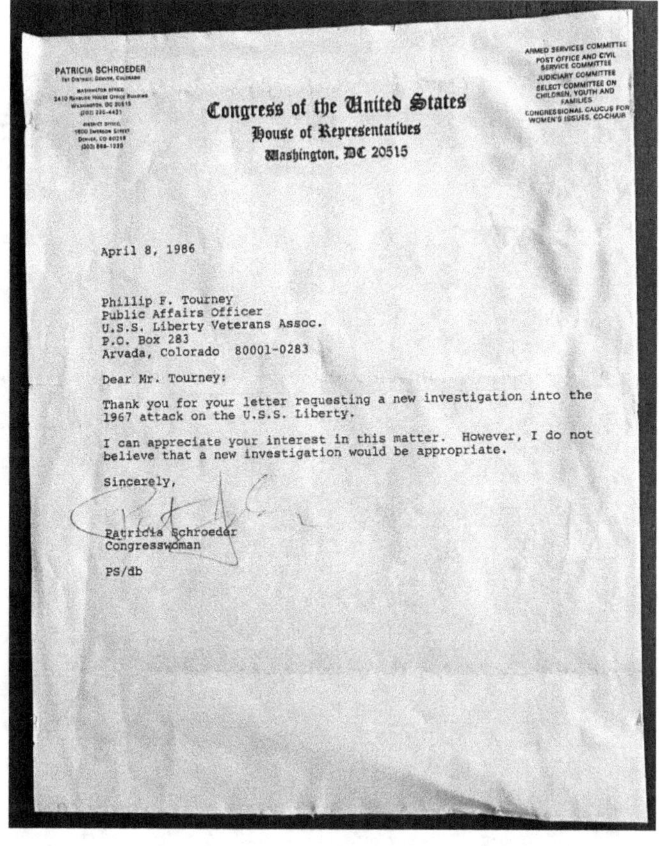

April 8, 1986

Phillip F. Tourney
Public Affairs Officer
U.S.S. Liberty Veterans Assoc.
P.O. Box 283
Arvada, Colorado 80001-0283

Dear Mr. Tourney:

Thank you for your letter requesting a new investigation into the 1967 attack on the U.S.S. Liberty.

I can appreciate your interest in this matter. However, I do not believe that a new investigation would be appropriate.

Sincerely,

Patricia Schroeder
Congresswoman

PS/db

Letter from Congressman Dan Schaefer, July 21, 1986

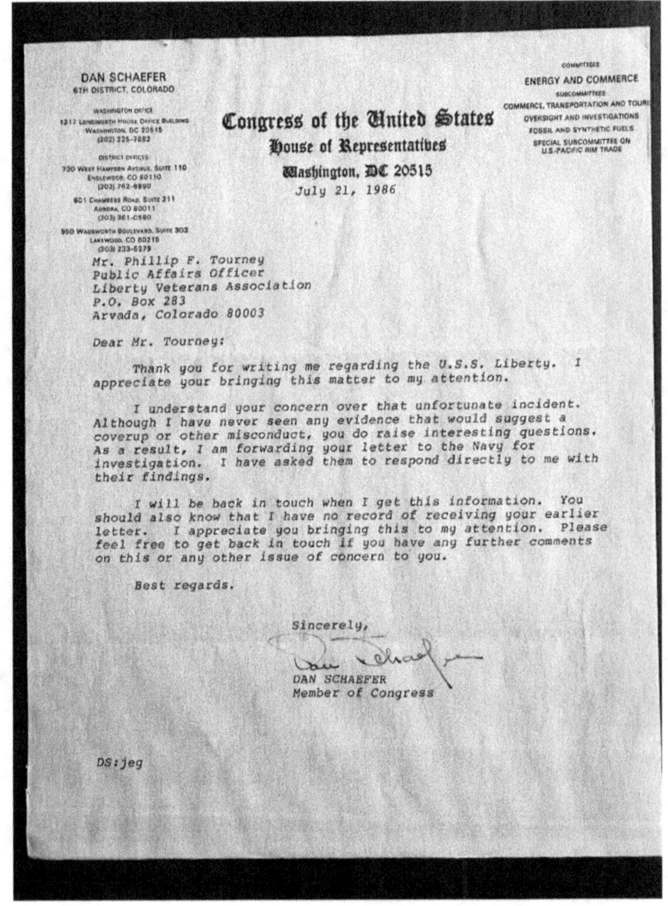

DAN SCHAEFER
6TH DISTRICT, COLORADO

WASHINGTON OFFICE
1317 LONGWORTH HOUSE OFFICE BUILDING
WASHINGTON, DC 20515
(202) 225-7882

DISTRICT OFFICES
730 WEST HAMPDEN AVENUE, SUITE 110
ENGLEWOOD, CO 80110
(303) 762-8890

601 CHAMBERS ROAD, SUITE 211
AURORA, CO 80011
(303) 361-0580

950 WADSWORTH BOULEVARD, SUITE 303
LAKEWOOD, CO 80215
(303) 233-5279

COMMITTEES
ENERGY AND COMMERCE
SUBCOMMITTEES
COMMERCE, TRANSPORTATION AND TOURISM
OVERSIGHT AND INVESTIGATIONS
FOSSIL AND SYNTHETIC FUELS
SPECIAL SUBCOMMITTEE ON
U.S.-PACIFIC RIM TRADE

Congress of the United States
House of Representatives
Washington, DC 20515

July 21, 1986

Mr. Phillip F. Tourney
Public Affairs Officer
Liberty Veterans Association
P.O. Box 283
Arvada, Colorado 80003

Dear Mr. Tourney:

Thank you for writing me regarding the U.S.S. Liberty. I appreciate your bringing this matter to my attention.

I understand your concern over that unfortunate incident. Although I have never seen any evidence that would suggest a coverup or other misconduct, you do raise interesting questions. As a result, I am forwarding your letter to the Navy for investigation. I have asked them to respond directly to me with their findings.

I will be back in touch when I get this information. You should also know that I have no record of receiving your earlier letter. I appreciate you bringing this to my attention. Please feel free to get back in touch if you have any further comments on this or any other issue of concern to you.

Best regards.

Sincerely,

DAN SCHAEFER
Member of Congress

DS:jeg

Another Letter from Congresswoman Patricia Schroeder, August 4, 1986

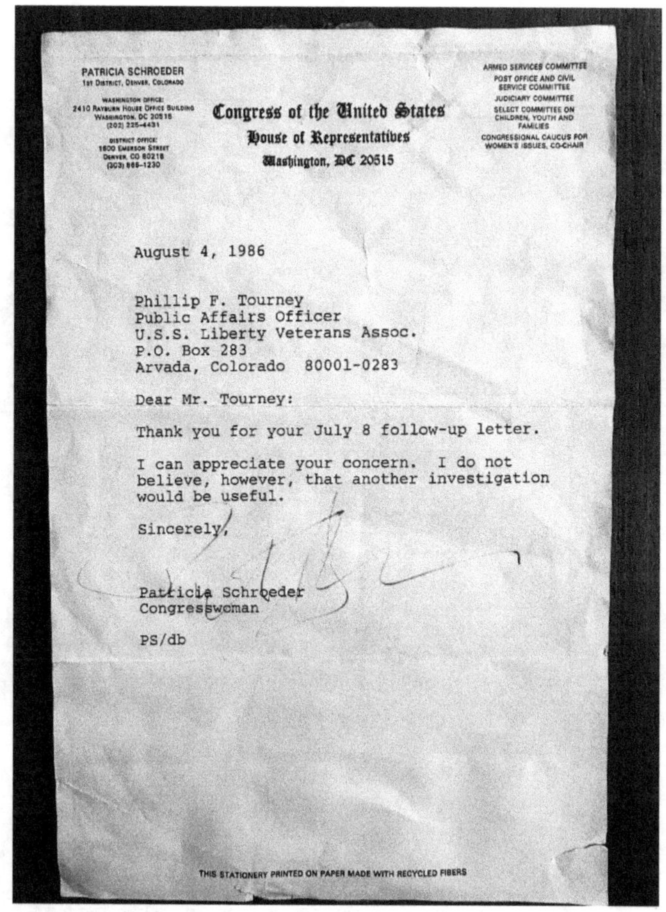

PATRICIA SCHROEDER
1st District, Denver, Colorado

WASHINGTON OFFICE:
2410 Rayburn House Office Building
Washington, DC 20515
(202) 225-4431

DISTRICT OFFICE:
1600 Emerson Street
Denver, CO 80218
(303) 866-1230

ARMED SERVICES COMMITTEE
POST OFFICE AND CIVIL
SERVICE COMMITTEE
JUDICIARY COMMITTEE
SELECT COMMITTEE ON
CHILDREN, YOUTH AND
FAMILIES
CONGRESSIONAL CAUCUS FOR
WOMEN'S ISSUES, CO-CHAIR

Congress of the United States
House of Representatives
Washington, DC 20515

August 4, 1986

Phillip F. Tourney
Public Affairs Officer
U.S.S. Liberty Veterans Assoc.
P.O. Box 283
Arvada, Colorado   80001-0283

Dear Mr. Tourney:

Thank you for your July 8 follow-up letter.

I can appreciate your concern. I do not
believe, however, that another investigation
would be useful.

Sincerely,

Patricia Schroeder
Congresswoman

PS/db

THIS STATIONERY PRINTED ON PAPER MADE WITH RECYCLED FIBERS

Another Letter from Congresswoman Patricia Schroeder to Marion Tourney, August 4, 1986

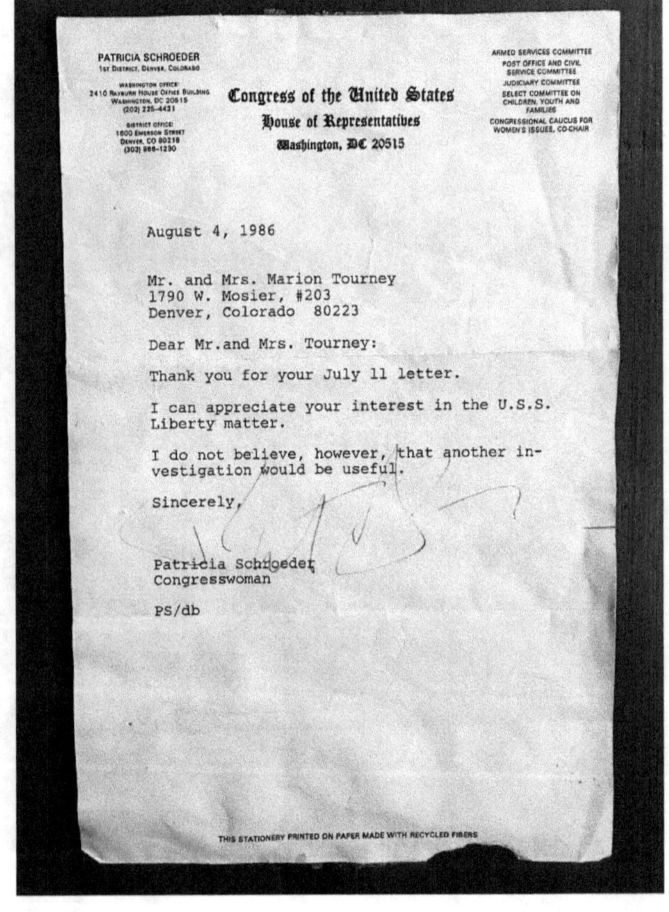

PATRICIA SCHROEDER
1st District, Denver, Colorado

WASHINGTON OFFICE:
2410 Rayburn House Office Building
Washington, DC 20515
(202) 225-4431

DISTRICT OFFICE:
1600 Emerson Street
Denver, CO 80218
(303) 866-1230

ARMED SERVICES COMMITTEE
POST OFFICE AND CIVIL SERVICE COMMITTEE
JUDICIARY COMMITTEE
SELECT COMMITTEE ON CHILDREN, YOUTH AND FAMILIES
CONGRESSIONAL CAUCUS FOR WOMEN'S ISSUES, CO-CHAIR

Congress of the United States
House of Representatives
Washington, DC 20515

August 4, 1986

Mr. and Mrs. Marion Tourney
1790 W. Mosier, #203
Denver, Colorado 80223

Dear Mr. and Mrs. Tourney:

Thank you for your July 11 letter.

I can appreciate your interest in the U.S.S. Liberty matter.

I do not believe, however, that another investigation would be useful.

Sincerely,

Patricia Schroeder
Congresswoman

PS/db

THIS STATIONERY PRINTED ON PAPER MADE WITH RECYCLED FIBERS

Letter from Congressman Ken Kramer,
August 5, 1986

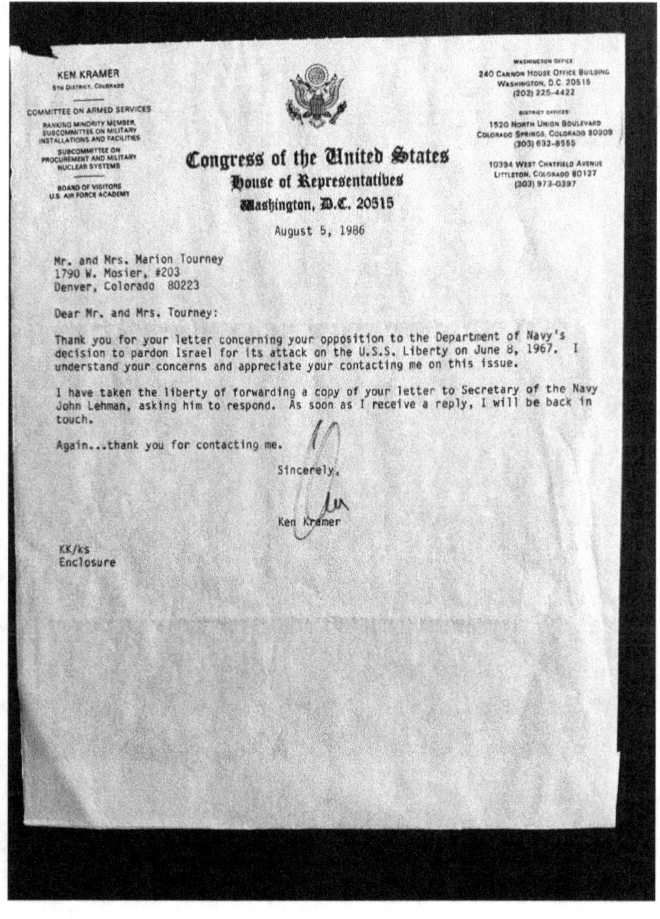

KEN KRAMER
5TH DISTRICT, COLORADO

COMMITTEE ON ARMED SERVICES

RANKING MINORITY MEMBER
SUBCOMMITTEE ON MILITARY
INSTALLATIONS AND FACILITIES
SUBCOMMITTEE ON
PROCUREMENT AND MILITARY
NUCLEAR SYSTEMS

BOARD OF VISITORS
U.S. AIR FORCE ACADEMY

WASHINGTON OFFICE:
240 CANNON HOUSE OFFICE BUILDING
WASHINGTON, D.C. 20515
(202) 225-4422

DISTRICT OFFICES:
1520 NORTH UNION BOULEVARD
COLORADO SPRINGS, COLORADO 80909
(303) 632-8555

10394 WEST CHATFIELD AVENUE
LITTLETON, COLORADO 80127
(303) 973-0397

Congress of the United States
House of Representatives
Washington, D.C. 20515

August 5, 1986

Mr. and Mrs. Marion Tourney
1790 W. Mosier, #203
Denver, Colorado 80223

Dear Mr. and Mrs. Tourney:

Thank you for your letter concerning your opposition to the Department of Navy's decision to pardon Israel for its attack on the U.S.S. Liberty on June 8, 1967. I understand your concerns and appreciate your contacting me on this issue.

I have taken the liberty of forwarding a copy of your letter to Secretary of the Navy John Lehman, asking him to respond. As soon as I receive a reply, I will be back in touch.

Again...thank you for contacting me.

Sincerely,

Ken Kramer

KK/ks
Enclosure

Letter from the American Educational Trust, November 16, 1986

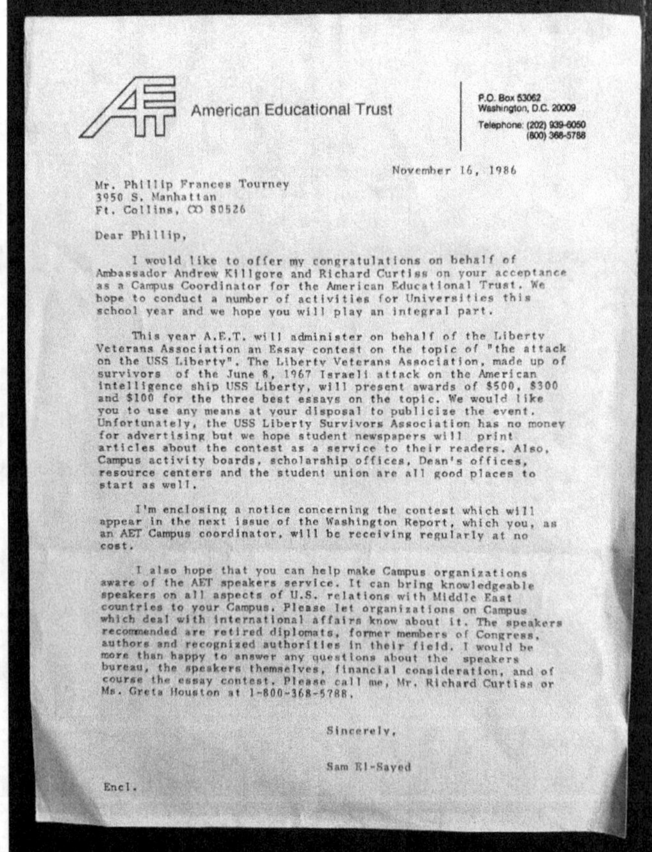

American Educational Trust

P.O. Box 53062
Washington, D.C. 20009
Telephone: (202) 939-6050
(800) 368-5788

November 16, 1986

Mr. Phillip Frances Tourney
3950 S. Manhattan
Ft. Collins, CO 80526

Dear Phillip,

I would like to offer my congratulations on behalf of Ambassador Andrew Killgore and Richard Curtiss on your acceptance as a Campus Coordinator for the American Educational Trust. We hope to conduct a number of activities for Universities this school year and we hope you will play an integral part.

This year A.E.T. will administer on behalf of the Liberty Veterans Association an Essay contest on the topic of "the attack on the USS Liberty". The Liberty Veterans Association, made up of survivors of the June 8, 1967 Israeli attack on the American intelligence ship USS Liberty, will present awards of $500, $300 and $100 for the three best essays on the topic. We would like you to use any means at your disposal to publicize the event. Unfortunately, the USS Liberty Survivors Association has no money for advertising but we hope student newspapers will print articles about the contest as a service to their readers. Also, Campus activity boards, scholarship offices, Dean's offices, resource centers and the student union are all good places to start as well.

I'm enclosing a notice concerning the contest which will appear in the next issue of the Washington Report, which you, as an AET Campus coordinator, will be receiving regularly at no cost.

I also hope that you can help make Campus organizations aware of the AET speakers service. It can bring knowledgeable speakers on all aspects of U.S. relations with Middle East countries to your Campus. Please let organizations on Campus which deal with international affairs know about it. The speakers recommended are retired diplomats, former members of Congress, authors and recognized authorities in their field. I would be more than happy to answer any questions about the speakers bureau, the speakers themselves, financial consideration, and of course the essay contest. Please call me, Mr. Richard Curtiss or Ms. Greta Houston at 1-800-368-5788.

Sincerely,

Sam El-Sayed

Encl.

Letter from the American Educational Trust, February 25, 1987

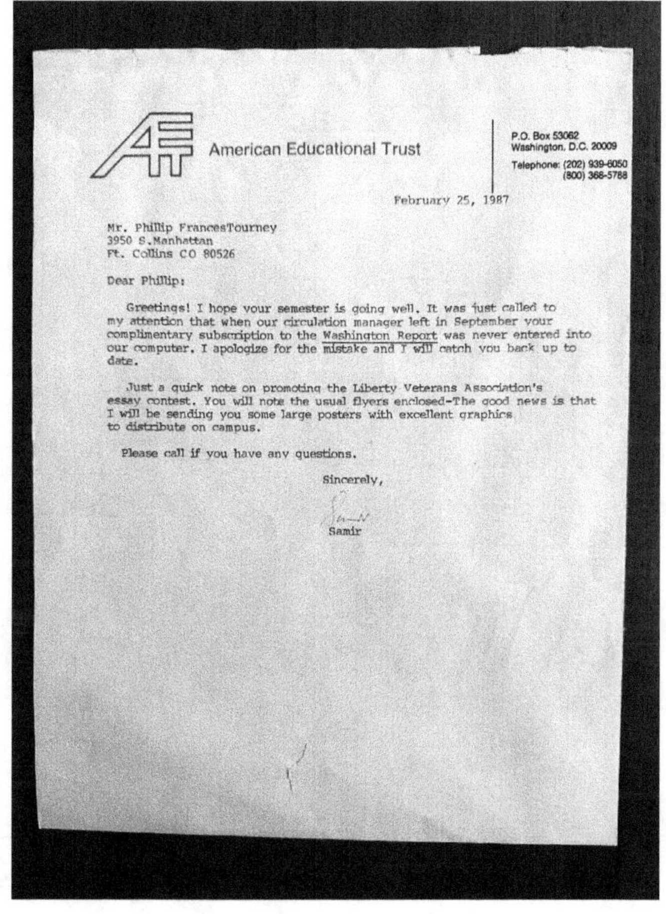

American Educational Trust

P.O. Box 53062
Washington, D.C. 20009

Telephone: (202) 939-6050
(800) 368-5788

February 25, 1987

Mr. Phillip FrancesTourney
3950 S.Manhattan
Ft. Collins CO 80526

Dear Phillip:

Greetings! I hope your semester is going well. It was just called to my attention that when our circulation manager left in September your complimentary subscription to the Washington Report was never entered into our computer. I apologize for the mistake and I will catch you back up to date.

Just a quick note on promoting the Liberty Veterans Association's essay contest. You will note the usual flyers enclosed—The good news is that I will be sending you some large posters with excellent graphics to distribute on campus.

Please call if you have any questions.

Sincerely,

Samir

Letter from Senator William L. Armstrong, June 8, 1987

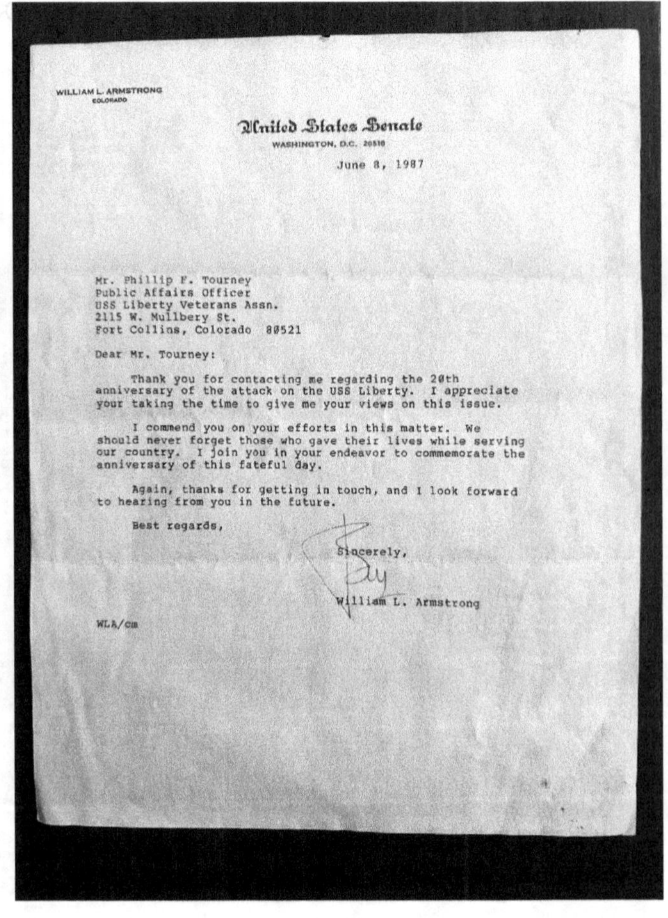

Another Letter from Congresswoman Patricia Schroeder, July 21, 1987

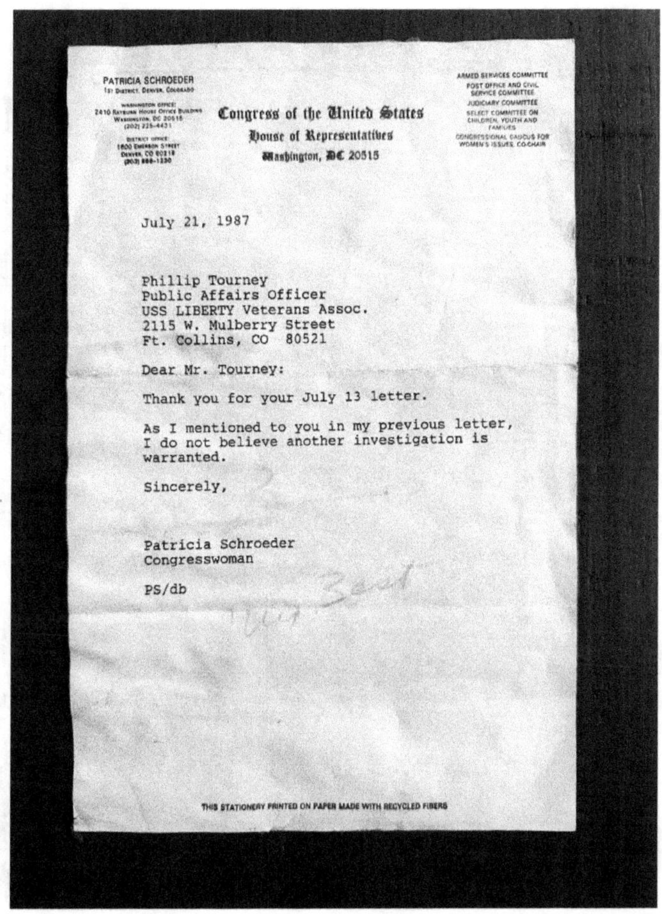

PATRICIA SCHROEDER
1st District, Denver, Colorado

WASHINGTON OFFICE:
2410 Rayburn House Office Building
Washington, DC 20515
(202) 225-4431

DISTRICT OFFICE:
1600 Emerson Street
Denver, CO 80218
(303) 866-1230

Congress of the United States
House of Representatives
Washington, DC 20515

ARMED SERVICES COMMITTEE
POST OFFICE AND CIVIL
SERVICE COMMITTEE
JUDICIARY COMMITTEE
SELECT COMMITTEE ON
CHILDREN, YOUTH AND
FAMILIES
CONGRESSIONAL CAUCUS FOR
WOMEN'S ISSUES, CO-CHAIR

July 21, 1987

Phillip Tourney
Public Affairs Officer
USS LIBERTY Veterans Assoc.
2115 W. Mulberry Street
Ft. Collins, CO 80521

Dear Mr. Tourney:

Thank you for your July 13 letter.

As I mentioned to you in my previous letter,
I do not believe another investigation is
warranted.

Sincerely,

Patricia Schroeder
Congresswoman

PS/db

THIS STATIONERY PRINTED ON PAPER MADE WITH RECYCLED FIBERS

Another Letter from Senator William L. Armstrong, August 5, 1987

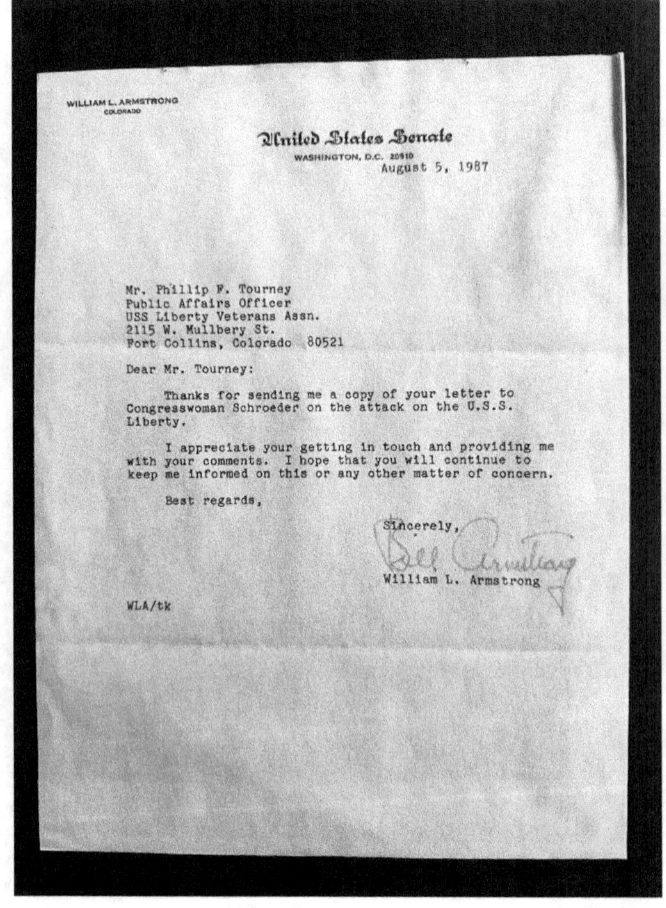

WILLIAM L. ARMSTRONG
COLORADO

United States Senate
WASHINGTON, D.C. 20510

August 5, 1987

Mr. Phillip F. Tourney
Public Affairs Officer
USS Liberty Veterans Assn.
2115 W. Mullbery St.
Fort Collins, Colorado 80521

Dear Mr. Tourney:

Thanks for sending me a copy of your letter to Congresswoman Schroeder on the attack on the U.S.S. Liberty.

I appreciate your getting in touch and providing me with your comments. I hope that you will continue to keep me informed on this or any other matter of concern.

Best regards,

Sincerely,

William L. Armstrong

WLA/tk

Letter from Congressman Hank Brown, August 21, 1987

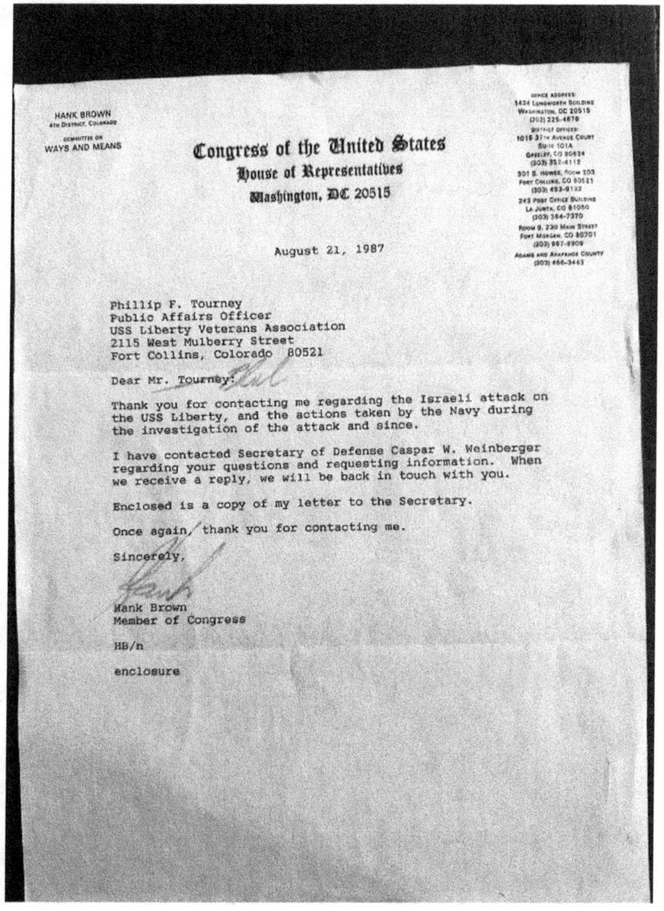

HANK BROWN
4TH DISTRICT, COLORADO

COMMITTEE ON
WAYS AND MEANS

OFFICE ADDRESS:
1424 LONGWORTH BUILDING
WASHINGTON, DC 20515
(202) 225-4676

DISTRICT OFFICES:
1015 37TH AVENUE COURT
SUITE 101A
GREELEY, CO 80634
(303) 352-4112

301 S. HOWES, ROOM 203
FORT COLLINS, CO 80521
(303) 493-9132

243 POST OFFICE BUILDING
LA JUNTA, CO 81050
(303) 384-7370

ROOM 9, 230 MAIN STREET
FORT MORGAN, CO 80701
(303) 867-8909

ADAMS AND ARAPAHOE COUNTY
(303) 466-3443

Congress of the United States
House of Representatives
Washington, DC 20515

August 21, 1987

Phillip F. Tourney
Public Affairs Officer
USS Liberty Veterans Association
2115 West Mulberry Street
Fort Collins, Colorado 80521

Dear Mr. Tourney:

Thank you for contacting me regarding the Israeli attack on
the USS Liberty, and the actions taken by the Navy during
the investigation of the attack and since.

I have contacted Secretary of Defense Caspar W. Weinberger
regarding your questions and requesting information. When
we receive a reply, we will be back in touch with you.

Enclosed is a copy of my letter to the Secretary.

Once again, thank you for contacting me.

Sincerely,

Hank Brown
Member of Congress

HB/n

enclosure

Letter from Senator Timothy E. Wirth, September 8, 1987

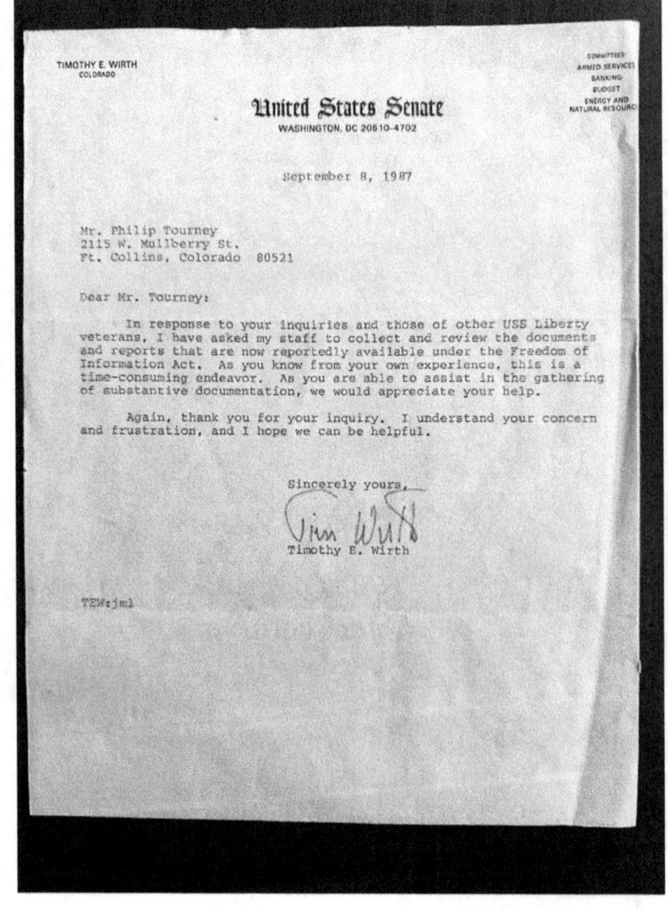

TIMOTHY E. WIRTH
COLORADO

COMMITTEES
ARMED SERVICES
BANKING
BUDGET
ENERGY AND
NATURAL RESOURCES

United States Senate
WASHINGTON, DC 20510-4702

September 8, 1987

Mr. Philip Tourney
2115 W. Mullberry St.
Ft. Collins, Colorado 80521

Dear Mr. Tourney:

In response to your inquiries and those of other USS Liberty veterans, I have asked my staff to collect and review the documents and reports that are now reportedly available under the Freedom of Information Act. As you know from your own experience, this is a time-consuming endeavor. As you are able to assist in the gathering of substantive documentation, we would appreciate your help.

Again, thank you for your inquiry. I understand your concern and frustration, and I hope we can be helpful.

Sincerely yours,

Timothy E. Wirth

TEW:jml

Letter from the Liberty Lobby, September 17, 1987

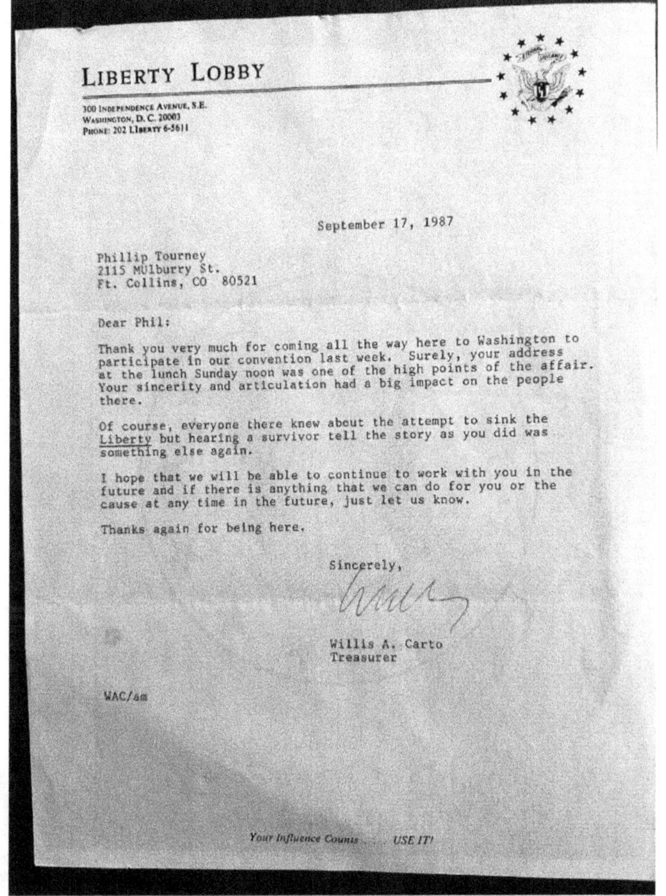

LIBERTY LOBBY

300 Independence Avenue, S.E.
Washington, D.C. 20003
Phone: 202 Liberty 6-5611

September 17, 1987

Phillip Tourney
2115 MUlburry St.
Ft. Collins, CO 80521

Dear Phil:

Thank you very much for coming all the way here to Washington to participate in our convention last week. Surely, your address at the lunch Sunday noon was one of the high points of the affair. Your sincerity and articulation had a big impact on the people there.

Of course, everyone there knew about the attempt to sink the Liberty but hearing a survivor tell the story as you did was something else again.

I hope that we will be able to continue to work with you in the future and if there is anything that we can do for you or the cause at any time in the future, just let us know.

Thanks again for being here.

Sincerely,

Willis A. Carto
Treasurer

WAC/am

Your Influence Counts . . . USE IT!

Letter from Congressman Hank Brown, October 13, 1987

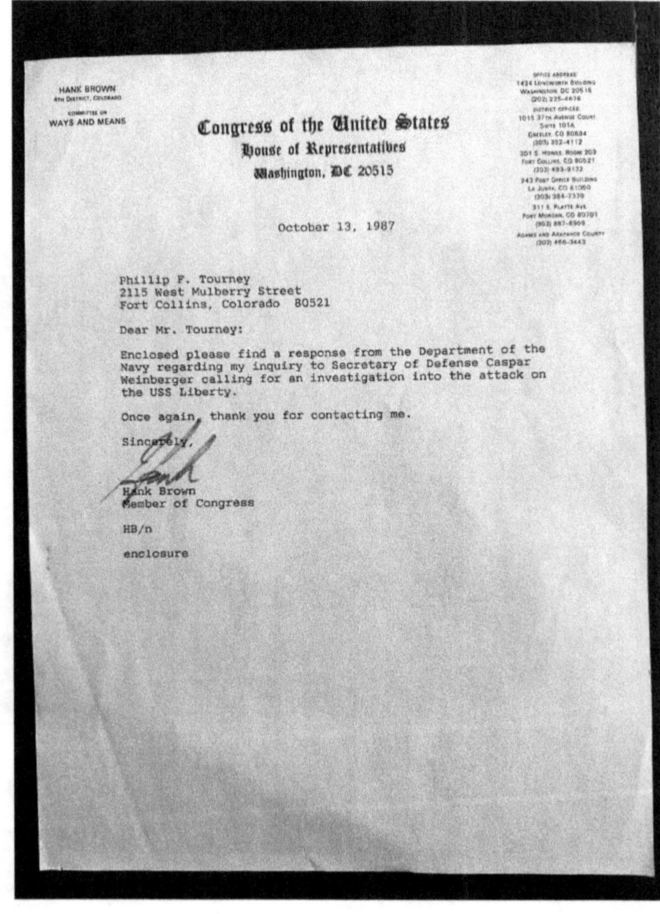

HANK BROWN
4TH DISTRICT, COLORADO

COMMITTEE ON
WAYS AND MEANS

Congress of the United States
House of Representatives
Washington, DC 20515

OFFICE ADDRESS
1424 LONGWORTH BUILDING
WASHINGTON, DC 20515
(202) 225-4676

DISTRICT OFFICES:
1015 37TH AVENUE COURT
Suite 101A
GREELEY, CO 80634
(303) 352-4112

301 S. HOWES, ROOM 203
FORT COLLINS, CO 80521
(303) 493-9133

743 POST OFFICE BUILDING
LA JUNTA, CO 81050
(303) 384-7370

311 S. PLATTE AVE.
FORT MORGAN, CO 80701
(303) 867-8909

ADAMS AND ARAPAHOE COUNTY
(303) 466-3443

October 13, 1987

Phillip F. Tourney
2115 West Mulberry Street
Fort Collins, Colorado 80521

Dear Mr. Tourney:

Enclosed please find a response from the Department of the
Navy regarding my inquiry to Secretary of Defense Caspar
Weinberger calling for an investigation into the attack on
the USS Liberty.

Once again, thank you for contacting me.

Sincerely,

Hank Brown
Member of Congress

HB/n

enclosure

Another Letter from Senator William L. Armstrong, February 25, 1988

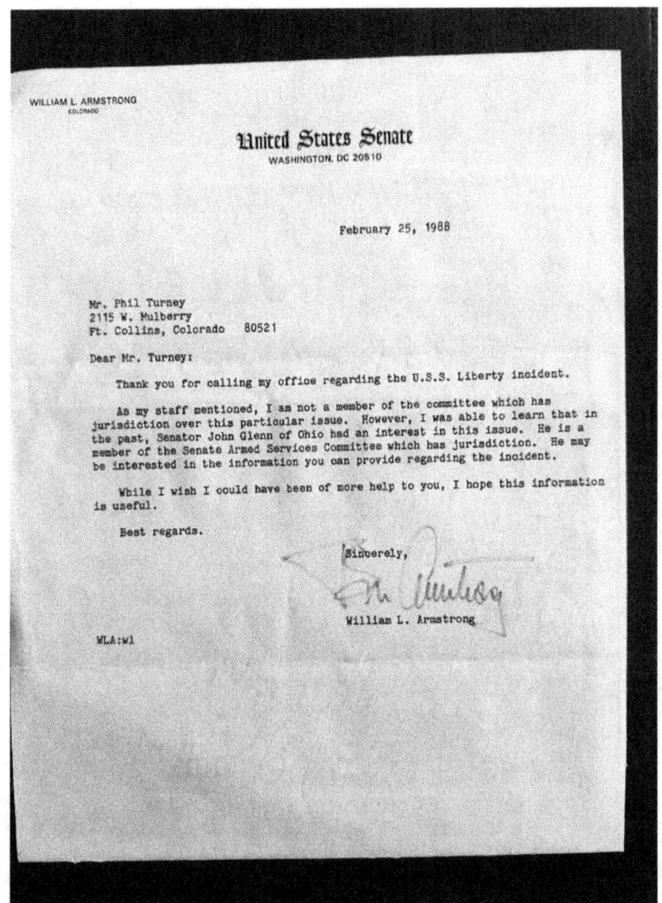

WILLIAM L. ARMSTRONG
COLORADO

United States Senate
WASHINGTON, DC 20510

February 25, 1988

Mr. Phil Turney
2115 W. Mulberry
Ft. Collins, Colorado   80521

Dear Mr. Turney:

Thank you for calling my office regarding the U.S.S. Liberty incident.

As my staff mentioned, I am not a member of the committee which has jurisdiction over this particular issue. However, I was able to learn that in the past, Senator John Glenn of Ohio had an interest in this issue. He is a member of the Senate Armed Services Committee which has jurisdiction. He may be interested in the information you can provide regarding the incident.

While I wish I could have been of more help to you, I hope this information is useful.

Best regards.

Sincerely,

William L. Armstrong

WLA:wl

Another Letter from Senator Timothy E. Wirth, March 7, 1988 – Page 1

United States Senate
WASHINGTON, D.C. 20510
March 7, 1988

Mr. Phil Tourney
2115 W. Mullberry St.
Fort Collins, Colorado 80521

Dear Mr. Tourney:

Thank you for writing to express your views on the unrest and violence which has plagued the West Bank and Gaza Strip since last December.

As you may know, I am a strong supporter of Israel. As a stable, democratic state, Israel is America's most reliable ally in an extremely unstable part of the globe. The turmoil within Lebanon, the continuing Iran-Iraq war, and the threat posed by Islamic fundamentalism all make our ties with Israel of extreme importance. The need to protect our security and economic interests in this vital region, as well as our deep moral commitment to the state of Israel, lead me to continue my support for this nation.

However, there are times when it is fully appropriate -- indeed, is obligatory -- for us to criticize the activities or policies of an ally. After weeks of violence in the occupied territories, much of it perpetrated by the Israeli military, now is just such a time. I am concerned that the policy of force, including the use of live ammunition and excessive violence, employed by the government of Israel to suppress the unrest in the West Bank and Gaza Strip seriously compromises Israel's proud democratic values and diminishes its credibility in the eyes of the world. More importantly, it exacerbates, rather than resolves, an already volatile situation.

The Reagan Administration has criticized Israel's recent activities, and encouraged Israel to ensure that the conduct of its military in the disputed region is consistent with accepted international standards. In addition, Secretary of State Shultz has proposed a new U.S. peace plan that calls for Israel and Jordan to agree on limited Palestinian self-rule in the West Bank and Gaza Strip, by September, with direct negotiations on the final status of the territories to follow in December.

I strongly support efforts to convince Israel and Jordan to negotiate directly with one another, and, in the interim, to press Israel to maintain control of the occupied territories in a humane way while improving conditions in the refugee camps. We will not

Letter from Senator Timothy E. Wirth, March 7, 1988 – Page 2

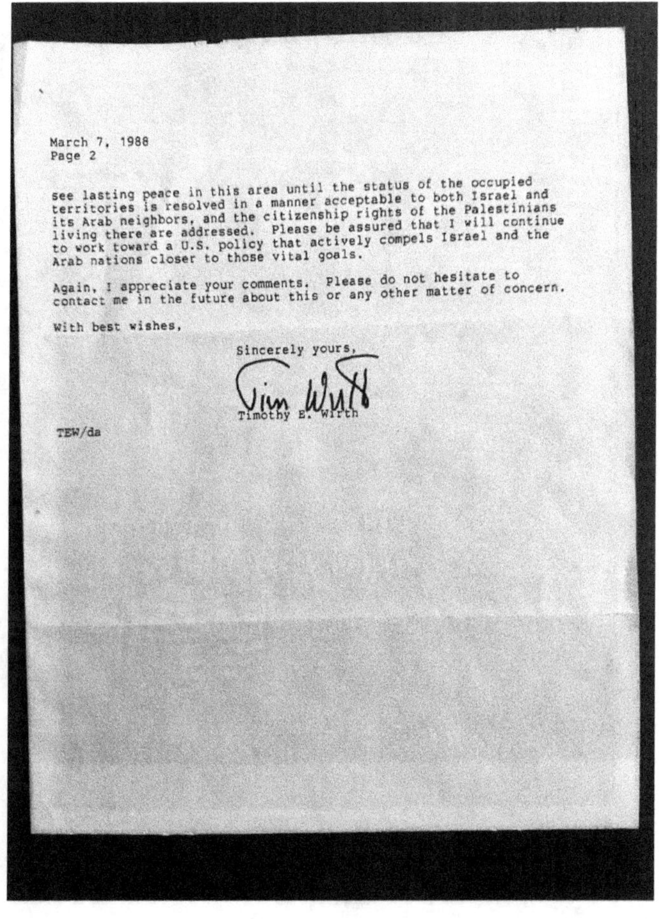

March 7, 1988
Page 2

see lasting peace in this area until the status of the occupied territories is resolved in a manner acceptable to both Israel and its Arab neighbors, and the citizenship rights of the Palestinians living there are addressed. Please be assured that I will continue to work toward a U.S. policy that actively compels Israel and the Arab nations closer to those vital goals.

Again, I appreciate your comments. Please do not hesitate to contact me in the future about this or any other matter of concern.

With best wishes,

Sincerely yours,

Timothy E. Wirth

TEW/da

Letter from Colorado State Representative Leo Jenkins, March 10, 1988

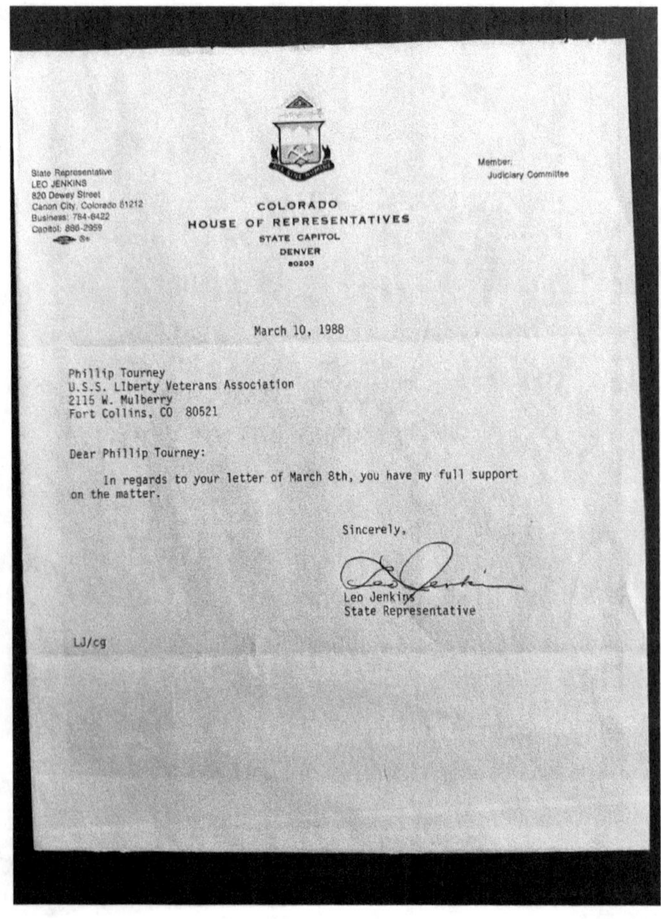

Another Letter from U.S. Senator Timothy E. Wirth, March 23, 1988

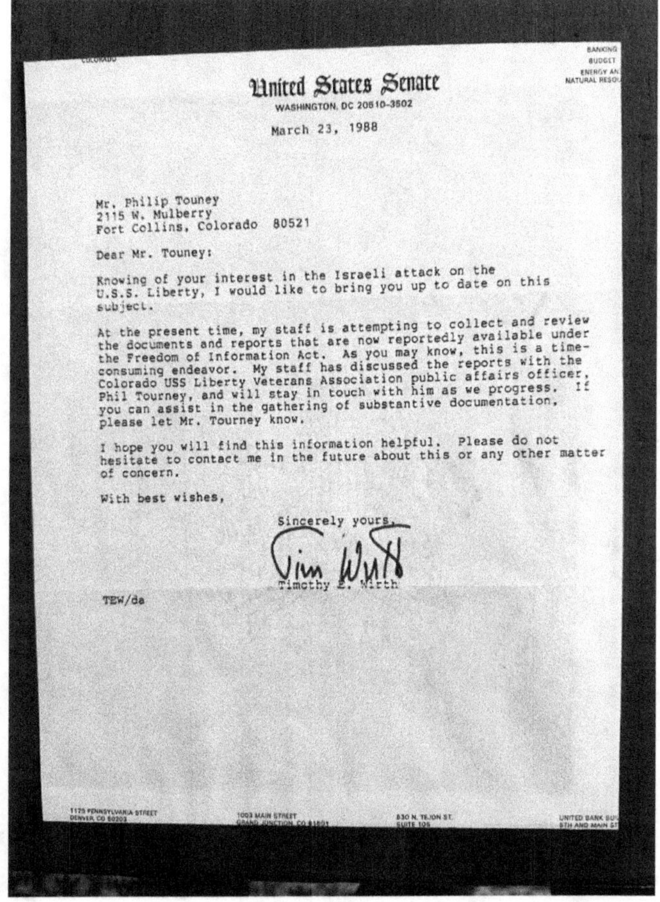

United States Senate
WASHINGTON, DC 20510-3502

March 23, 1988

Mr. Philip Touney
2115 W. Mulberry
Fort Collins, Colorado 80521

Dear Mr. Touney:

Knowing of your interest in the Israeli attack on the U.S.S. Liberty, I would like to bring you up to date on this subject.

At the present time, my staff is attempting to collect and review the documents and reports that are now reportedly available under the Freedom of Information Act. As you may know, this is a time-consuming endeavor. My staff has discussed the reports with the Colorado USS Liberty Veterans Association public affairs officer, Phil Tourney, and will stay in touch with him as we progress. If you can assist in the gathering of substantive documentation, please let Mr. Tourney know.

I hope you will find this information helpful. Please do not hesitate to contact me in the future about this or any other matter of concern.

With best wishes,

Sincerely yours,

Timothy E. Wirth

TEW/da

Another Letter from U.S. Senator William L. Armstrong, May 5, 1988

WILLIAM L. ARMSTRONG
COLORADO

United States Senate
WASHINGTON, D.C. 20510

May 5, 1988

Mr. Phillip F. Tourney
Public Affairs Officer
USS Liberty Veterans Assn.
2115 W. Mullbery St.
Fort Collins, Colorado 80521

Dear Mr. Tourney:

Thank you for contacting me about the 1967 attack on the U.S.S. Liberty.

Many people have contacted me regarding this situation, and I can well understand your desire to have the facts on this issue. I am aware of the incident and the many investigations which have taken place over the years. I appreciate your taking the time to give me your suggestions on this subject, and thank you again for getting in touch.

Please stay in touch.

Best regards,

Sincerely,

William L. Armstrong

WLA/jm

P.S. Thanks also for your thoughts about Israel. I support continued aid to Israel to help stabilize the situation in that region.

Another Letter from U.S. Congressman Hank Brown, May 6, 1988

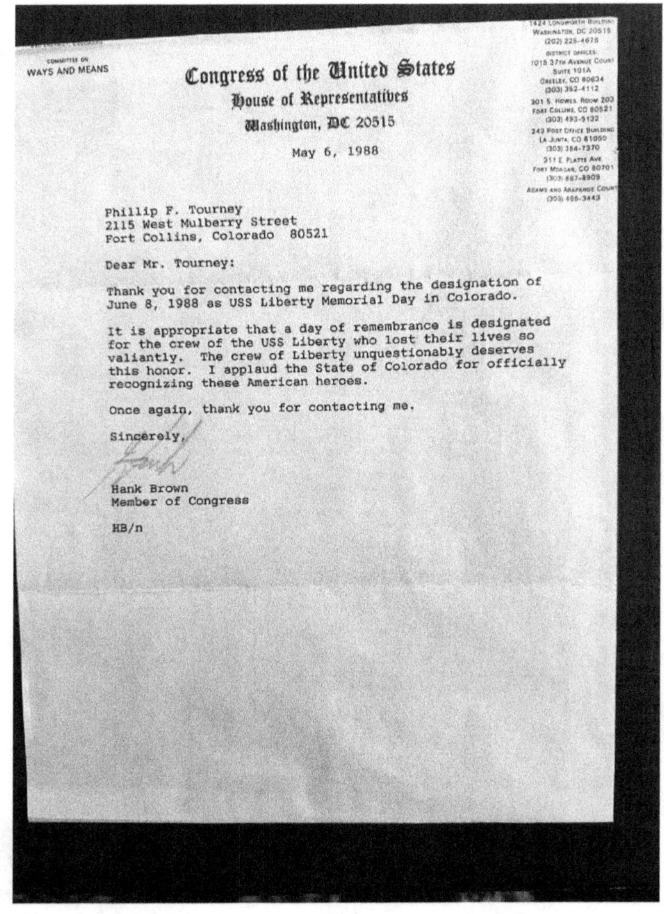

Congress of the United States
House of Representatives
Washington, DC 20515

May 6, 1988

Phillip F. Tourney
2115 West Mulberry Street
Fort Collins, Colorado 80521

Dear Mr. Tourney:

Thank you for contacting me regarding the designation of June 8, 1988 as USS Liberty Memorial Day in Colorado.

It is appropriate that a day of remembrance is designated for the crew of the USS Liberty who lost their lives so valiantly. The crew of Liberty unquestionably deserves this honor. I applaud the State of Colorado for officially recognizing these American heroes.

Once again, thank you for contacting me.

Sincerely,

Hank Brown
Member of Congress

HB/n

Letter from U.S. Senator Edward M. Kennedy, July 6, 1988

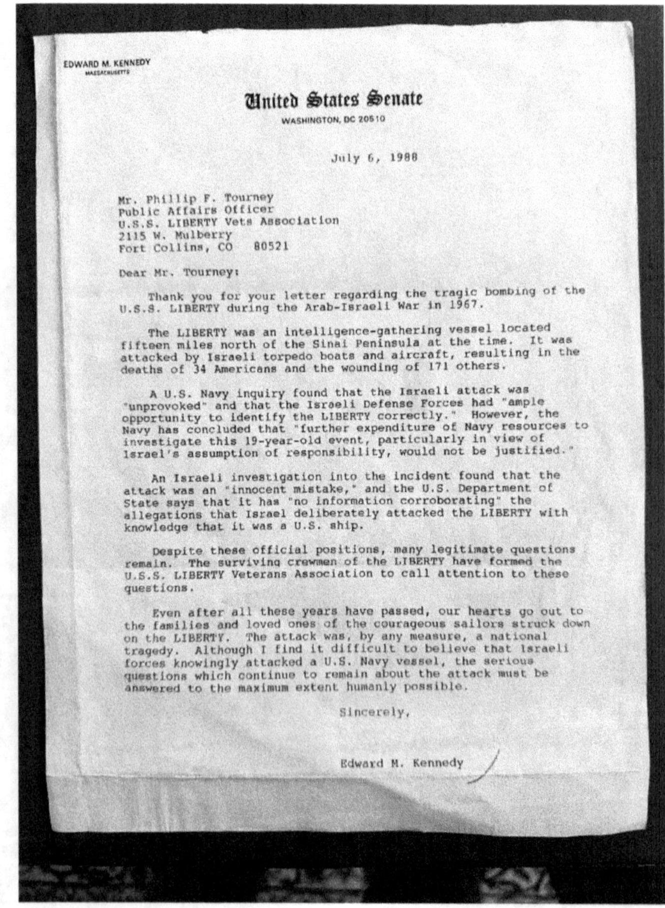

EDWARD M. KENNEDY
MASSACHUSETTS

United States Senate
WASHINGTON, DC 20510

July 6, 1988

Mr. Phillip F. Tourney
Public Affairs Officer
U.S.S. LIBERTY Vets Association
2115 W. Mulberry
Fort Collins, CO   80521

Dear Mr. Tourney:

Thank you for your letter regarding the tragic bombing of the U.S.S. LIBERTY during the Arab-Israeli War in 1967.

The LIBERTY was an intelligence-gathering vessel located fifteen miles north of the Sinai Peninsula at the time. It was attacked by Israeli torpedo boats and aircraft, resulting in the deaths of 34 Americans and the wounding of 171 others.

A U.S. Navy inquiry found that the Israeli attack was "unprovoked" and that the Israeli Defense Forces had "ample opportunity to identify the LIBERTY correctly." However, the Navy has concluded that "further expenditure of Navy resources to investigate this 19-year-old event, particularly in view of Israel's assumption of responsibility, would not be justified."

An Israeli investigation into the incident found that the attack was an "innocent mistake," and the U.S. Department of State says that it has "no information corroborating" the allegations that Israel deliberately attacked the LIBERTY with knowledge that it was a U.S. ship.

Despite these official positions, many legitimate questions remain. The surviving crewmen of the LIBERTY have formed the U.S.S. LIBERTY Veterans Association to call attention to these questions.

Even after all these years have passed, our hearts go out to the families and loved ones of the courageous sailors struck down on the LIBERTY. The attack was, by any measure, a national tragedy. Although I find it difficult to believe that Israeli forces knowingly attacked a U.S. Navy vessel, the serious questions which continue to remain about the attack must be answered to the maximum extent humanly possible.

Sincerely,

Edward M. Kennedy

Letter from Admiral Thomas H. Moorer (Ret.), January 4, 1989

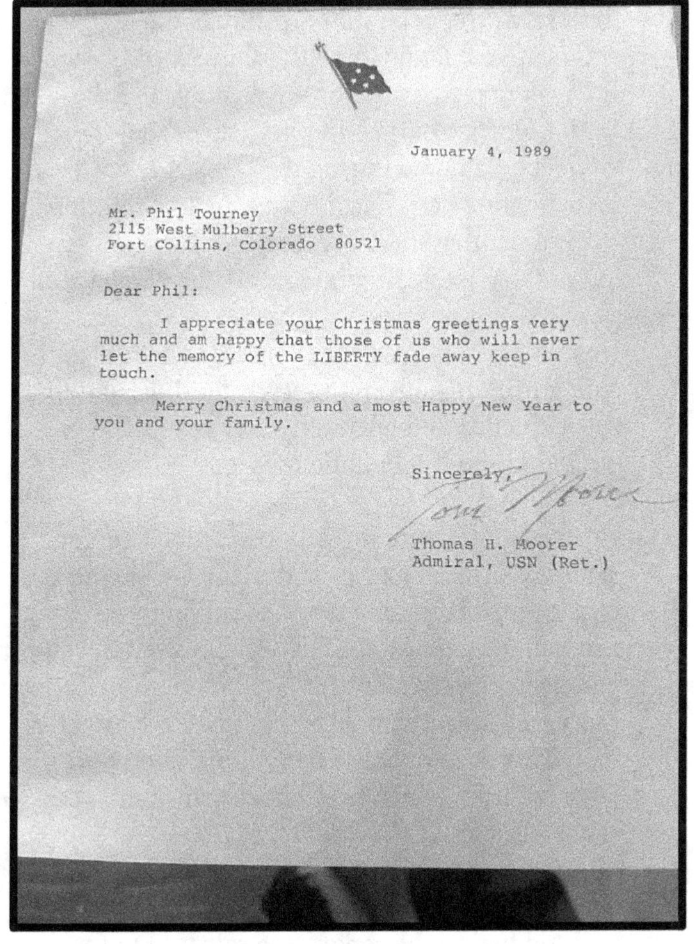

January 4, 1989

Mr. Phil Tourney
2115 West Mulberry Street
Fort Collins, Colorado 80521

Dear Phil:

I appreciate your Christmas greetings very much and am happy that those of us who will never let the memory of the LIBERTY fade away keep in touch.

Merry Christmas and a most Happy New Year to you and your family.

Sincerely,

Thomas H. Moorer
Admiral, USN (Ret.)

Declaration of Captain Ward Boston, Jr., January 8, 2004

In this sworn declaration, former Navy Judge Advocate General Corps Captain Ward Boston, Jr., who served as senior legal counsel to the **USS *Liberty*** Court of Inquiry, states that the evidence gathered during the Navy's investigation convinced both him and Admiral Isaac Kidd that the 1967 attack on the *Liberty* was deliberate rather than accidental.

Boston further asserts that orders constrained the official findings from higher authorities and that key evidence and testimony were excluded or altered in the final public record.

Boston's statement directly challenges the long-standing official narrative that the attack was a case of mistaken identity. According to his account, the investigative team believed the ship had been clearly identified as American and that the attack was planned. Still, they were given only a week to conduct the inquiry and were later told to reach a different conclusion.

His declaration also claims that portions of the original testimony and findings were altered or omitted before the report was released to the public, reinforcing the belief among many survivors and investigators that the full truth of the incident was suppressed.

Read his sworn declaration in its entirety here:

DECLARATION OF WARD BOSTON, JR., CAPTAIN, JAGC, USN (RET.)

I, WARD BOSTON, JR. DO DECLARE THAT THE FOLLOWING STATEMENT IS TRUE AND COMPLETE:

1.   FOR MORE THAN 30 YEARS, I HAVE REMAINED SILENT ON THE TOPIC OF USS *LIBERTY*. I AM A MILITARY MAN AND WHEN ORDERS COME IN FROM THE SECRETARY OF DEFENSE AND PRESIDENT OF THE UNITED STATES, I FOLLOW THEM.

2.   HOWEVER, RECENT ATTEMPTS TO REWRITE HISTORY COMPEL ME TO SHARE THE TRUTH.

3.   IN JUNE OF 1967, WHILE SERVING AS A CAPTAIN IN THE Judge Advocate General Corps, Department of the Navy, I WAS ASSIGNED AS SENIOR LEGAL COUNSEL FOR THE NAVY'S COURT OF INQUIRY INTO THE BRUTAL ATTACK ON USS *LIBERTY*, WHICH HAD OCCURRED ON JUNE 8TH.

4.   THE LATE ADMIRAL ISAAC C. KIDD, PRESIDENT OF THE COURT, AND I WERE GIVEN ONLY ONE WEEK TO GATHER EVIDENCE FOR THE NAVY'S OFFICIAL INVESTIGATION INTO THE ATTACK, DESPITE THE FACT THAT WE BOTH HAD ESTIMATED THAT A PROPER COURT OF INQUIRY INTO AN ATTACK OF THIS MAGNITUDE WOULD TAKE AT LEAST SIX MONTHS TO CONDUCT.

5.   ADMIRAL JOHN S. McCAIN, JR., THEN COMMANDER-IN-CHIEF, NAVAL FORCES EUROPE (CINCUSNAVEUR), AT HIS HEADQUARTERS IN LONDON, HAD CHARGED ADMIRAL KIDD (IN A LETTER DATED JUNE 10, 1967) TO

> "INQUIRE INTO ALL THE PERTINENT FACTS AND CIRCUMSTANCES LEADING TO
> AND CONNECTED WITH THE ARMED ATTACK; DAMAGE RESULTING THEREFROM; AND DEATHS OF AND INJURIES TO NAVAL PERSONNEL."

6.   DESPITE THE SHORT AMOUNT OF TIME WE WERE GIVEN, WE GATHERED A VAST AMOUNT OF EVIDENCE, INCLUDING HOURS OF HEARTBREAKING TESTIMONY FROM THE YOUNG SURVIVORS.

7.   THE EVIDENCE WAS CLEAR. BOTH ADMIRAL KIDD AND I BELIEVED WITH CERTAINTY THAT THIS ATTACK, WHICH KILLED 34 AMERICAN SAILORS AND INJURED 172 OTHERS, WAS A DELIBERATE EFFORT TO SINK AN AMERICAN SHIP AND MURDER ITS ENTIRE CREW. EACH EVENING, AFTER HEARING TESTIMONY ALL DAY, WE OFTEN SPOKE OUR PRIVATE THOUGHTS CONCERNING WHAT WE HAD SEEN AND HEARD. I RECALL ADMIRAL KIDD REPEATEDLY REFERRING TO THE ISRAELI FORCES RESPONSIBLE FOR THE ATTACK AS "MURDEROUS BASTARDS." IT WAS OUR SHARED BELIEF, BASED ON THE DOCUMENTARY EVIDENCE AND TESTIMONY WE RE-

Declaration of Ward Boston, Jr., Captain, JAGC, USN (Ret.) – Page 1 of 4

1 CEIVED FIRST HAND, THAT THE ISRAELI ATTACK WAS PLANNED AND DELIBERATE, AND COULD NOT POSSIBLY

2 HAVE BEEN AN ACCIDENT.

3 8.   I AM CERTAIN THAT THE ISRAELI PILOTS THAT UNDERTOOK THE ATTACK, AS WELL AS THEIR SUPERIORS,

4 WHO HAD ORDERED THE ATTACK, WERE WELL AWARE THAT THE SHIP WAS AMERICAN.

5 9.   I SAW THE FLAG, WHICH HAD VISIBLY IDENTIFIED THE SHIP AS AMERICAN, RIDDLED WITH BULLET

6 HOLES, AND HEARD TESTIMONY THAT MADE IT CLEAR THAT THE ISRAELIS INTENDED THERE BE NO SURVIVORS.

7 10.   NOT ONLY DID THE ISRAELIS ATTACK THE SHIP WITH NAPALM, GUNFIRE, AND MISSILES, ISRAELI TOR-

8 PEDO BOATS MACHINE-GUNNED THREE LIFEBOATS THAT HAD BEEN LAUNCHED IN AN ATTEMPT BY THE CREW

9 TO SAVE THE MOST SERIOUSLY WOUNDED – A WAR CRIME.

10 11.   ADMIRAL KIDD AND I BOTH FELT IT NECESSARY TO TRAVEL TO ISRAEL TO INTERVIEW THE ISRAELIS

11 WHO TOOK PART IN THE ATTACK. ADMIRAL KIDD TELEPHONED ADMIRAL MCCAIN TO DISCUSS MAKING AR-

12 RANGEMENTS. ADMIRAL KIDD LATER TOLD ME THAT ADMIRAL MCCAIN WAS ADAMANT THAT WE WERE NOT

13 TO TRAVEL TO ISRAEL OR CONTACT THE ISRAELIS CONCERNING THIS MATTER.

14 12.   REGRETTABLY, WE DID NOT RECEIVE INTO EVIDENCE AND THE COURT DID NOT CONSIDER ANY OF

15 THE MORE THAN SIXTY WITNESS DECLARATIONS FROM MEN WHO HAD BEEN HOSPITALIZED AND WERE UNABLE

16 TO TESTIFY IN PERSON.

17 13.   I AM OUTRAGED AT THE EFFORTS OF THE APOLOGISTS FOR ISRAEL IN THIS COUNTRY TO CLAIM THAT

18 THIS ATTACK WAS A CASE OF "MISTAKEN IDENTITY."

19 14.   IN PARTICULAR, THE RECENT PUBLICATION OF JAY CRISTOL'S BOOK, *THE LIBERTY INCIDENT*, TWISTS

20 THE FACTS AND MISREPRESENTS THE VIEWS OF THOSE OF US WHO INVESTIGATED THE ATTACK.

21 15.   IT IS CRISTOL'S INSIDIOUS ATTEMPT TO WHITEWASH THE FACTS THAT HAS PUSHED ME TO SPEAK OUT.

22 16.   I KNOW FROM PERSONAL CONVERSATIONS I HAD WITH ADMIRAL KIDD THAT PRESIDENT LYNDON

23 JOHNSON AND SECRETARY OF DEFENSE ROBERT MCNAMARA ORDERED HIM TO CONCLUDE THAT THE AT-

24 TACK WAS A CASE OF "MISTAKEN IDENTITY" DESPITE OVERWHELMING EVIDENCE TO THE CONTRARY.

25 17.   ADMIRAL KIDD TOLD ME, AFTER RETURNING FROM WASHINGTON, D.C. THAT HE HAD BEEN OR-

26 DERED TO SIT DOWN WITH TWO CIVILIANS FROM EITHER THE WHITE HOUSE OR THE DEFENSE DEPARTMENT,

27 AND REWRITE PORTIONS OF THE COURT'S FINDINGS.

28

Declaration of Ward Boston, Jr., Captain, JAGC, USN (Ret.) – Page 2 of 4

1 18.   Admiral Kidd also told me that he had been ordered to "put the lid" on everything hav-
2 ing to do with the attack on USS Liberty. We were never to speak of it and we were to caution
3 everyone else involved that they could never speak of it again.

4 19.   I have no reason to doubt the accuracy of that statement as I know that the Court of
5 Inquiry transcript that has been released to the public is not the same one that I certified and
6 sent off to Washington.

7 20.   I know this because it was necessary, due to the exigencies of time, to hand correct
8 and initial a substantial number of pages. I have examined the released version of the tran-
9 script and I did not see any pages that bore my hand corrections and initials. Also, the origi-
10 nal did not have any deliberately blank pages, as the released version does. Finally, the testi-
11 mony of Lt. Painter concerning the deliberate machine gunning of the life rafts by the Israeli
12 torpedo boat crews, which I distinctly recall being given at the Court of Inquiry and in-
13 cluded in the original transcript, is now missing and has been excised.

14 21.   Following the conclusion of the Court of Inquiry, Admiral Kidd and I remained in
15 contact. Though we never spoke of the attack in public, we did discuss it between ourselves,
16 on occasion. Every time we discussed the attack, Admiral Kidd was adamant that it was a de-
17 liberate, planned attack on an American ship.

18 22.   In 1990, I received a telephone call from Jay Cristol, who wanted to interview me
19 concerning the functioning of the Court of Inquiry. I told him that I would not speak to him
20 on that subject and prepared to hang up the telephone. Cristol then began asking me about
21 my personal background and other, non-Court of Inquiry related matters. I endeavored to
22 answer these questions and politely extricate myself from the conversation. Cristol contin-
23 ued to return to the subject of the Court of Inquiry, which I refused to discuss with him. Fi-
24 nally, I suggested that he contact Admiral Kidd and ask him about the Court of Inquiry.

25 23.   Shortly after my conversation with Cristol, I received a telephone call from Admiral
26 Kidd, inquiring about Cristol and what he was up to. The Admiral spoke of Cristol in dispar-
27 aging terms and even opined that "Cristol must be an Israeli agent." I don't know if he meant
28

1   THAT LITERALLY OR IT WAS HIS WAY OF EXPRESSING HIS DISGUST FOR CRISTOL'S HIGHLY PARTISAN, PRO-

2   ISRAELI APPROACH TO QUESTIONS INVOLVING *USS LIBERTY*.

3   24.   AT NO TIME DID I EVER HEAR ADMIRAL KIDD SPEAK OF CRISTOL OTHER THAN IN HIGHLY DISPARAG-

4   ING TERMS. I FIND CRISTOL'S CLAIMS OF A "CLOSE FRIENDSHIP" WITH ADMIRAL KIDD TO BE UTTERLY IN-

5   CREDIBLE. I ALSO FIND IT IMPOSSIBLE TO BELIEVE THE STATEMENTS HE ATTRIBUTES TO ADMIRAL KIDD, CON-

6   CERNING THE ATTACK ON *USS LIBERTY*.

7   25.   SEVERAL YEARS LATER, I RECEIVED A LETTER FROM CRISTOL THAT CONTAINED WHAT HE PURPORTED

8   TO BE HIS NOTES OF OUR PRIOR CONVERSATION. THESE "NOTES" WERE GROSSLY INCORRECT AND BORE NO

9   RESEMBLANCE IN REALITY TO THAT DISCUSSION. I FIND IT HARD TO BELIEVE THAT THESE "NOTES" WERE THE

10   PRODUCT OF A MISTAKE, RATHER THAN AN ATTEMPT TO DECEIVE. I INFORMED CRISTOL THAT I DISAGREED

11   WITH HIS RECOLLECTION OF OUR CONVERSATION AND THAT HE WAS WRONG. CRISTOL MADE SEVERAL AT-

12   TEMPTS TO ARRANGE FOR THE TWO OF US TO MEET IN PERSON AND TALK BUT I ALWAYS FOUND WAYS TO

13   AVOID DOING THIS. I DID NOT WISH TO MEET WITH CRISTOL AS WE HAD NOTHING IN COMMON AND I DID

14   NOT TRUST HIM.

15   26.   CONTRARY TO THE MISINFORMATION PRESENTED BY CRISTOL AND OTHERS, IT IS IMPORTANT FOR THE

16   AMERICAN PEOPLE TO KNOW THAT IT IS CLEAR THAT ISRAEL IS RESPONSIBLE FOR DELIBERATELY ATTACKING

17   AN AMERICAN SHIP AND MURDERING AMERICAN SAILORS, WHOSE BEREAVED SHIPMATES HAVE LIVED WITH

18   THIS EGREGIOUS CONCLUSION FOR MANY YEARS.

19   DATED: JANUARY 8, 2004

20   AT CORONADO, CALIFORNIA.

21

22   WARD BOSTON, JR., CAPTAIN, JAGC, USN (RET.)

23   SENIOR COUNSEL TO THE USS LIBERTY COURT OF INQUIRY

24

25

26

27

28

Declaration of Ward Boston, Jr., Captain, JAGC, USN (Ret.) – Page 4 of 4